THE TROJAN HORSE
OF LEADERSHIP

Battling the Enemy We All Face

Jon Korkidakis

Cover Artwork by Chantal Carrier
Cover Design by Kent Weber, Jason and Suzanne Korkidakis

ACKNOWLEDGEMENTS

Every writer who has taken the journey towards completing a manuscript knows that the trip is rarely made alone. Many contribute and the journey becomes peppered with the faces and unique touches of those who have impacted the road in one way or another.

To Village Green Community Church, thank you for the privilege of serving you as your pastor. From the Elders, Board of Directors, Staff, and Congregation, you have made it a pleasure to share life and ministry together.

To Heritage College and Seminary; since 1996 you have given me a platform to engage future leaders and help prepare them for a life of service. I am especially indebted to Dr. David Barker for taking a chance on me those many years ago.

To Kent and Carolyn Weber; I've yet to meet a couple more dynamic than you. Separate you are a whirlwind of inspiration, but together a true force of nature. Thank you for the way you helped carry this project to fruition and the many nights of pizza, strategy, laughter, and more pizza.

To Rheba Moore-Nash; no manuscript of worth could ever be so counted without the deftness of your grammatical touch. This book is far better because of the time you took to make it so.

To Chantal Carrier; when an artist's touch was required, there was no better person to turn to but you.

To Peter Kryshtalovich for your thoughtful wisdom and strength of foresight. You gave me what I needed when the well was dry. Some of the more profound thoughts came from conversations we shared, a hallmark of our ongoing friendship.

To my sons, Michael and Jason; to call you cheerleaders would diminish the extent in which you have both come alongside and carried me when needed. You kept the flame alive as it were, and I'm grateful for the men you've become. Suzanne, you too deserve acknowledgment for becoming a shared voice of encouragement. Something that was evident the moment you joined our family.

No one has provoked me to exercise my talents more profoundly than my wife Darlene. Thirty-one years of marriage does not one make without recognizing the contributions of a spouse. You have made every part of my life better, especially those areas most lacking refinement. Your support and strength have kept me going and it has made this book possible through your sheer encouragement and perseverance.

To all the leaders whose lives I hope this book will touch. May you gain insight into your strengths and how to guard them, not only for the sake of self-improvement, but for the sake of every soul you lead.

TABLE OF CONTENTS

INTRODUCTION

Who asks whether the enemy was defeated by strategy or valor? Virgil

O' the mass of arms, the brilliant leadership, the courage and magnitude of the ancient armies of Greece, combined to conquer the city of Troy - all that, and ten years of perseverance. Hipponax The Satirist quotes

The war had raged for ten years. Two enemies battled ferociously upon the plains before a fabled city. Each side immortalizing the names of warriors who fought a war that never seemed to end. Achilles, Hector, Agamemnon, Odysseus, Priam, heroes who had gathered to fight on the pretense of one man's honor, Menelaus, whose wife Helen was taken by the Trojan, Paris.

The Trojan War is one of history's most legendary and notable battles. Even now, it evokes images of a time when heroes rallied for a cause, even if it meant certain death. For the honor of one's name, to die in battle brought glory beyond a reclusive life lived in anonymity. Victory was therefore paramount, and each side had its own reasons for winning.

After ten years of warring, the promise of victory for the Greeks appeared to be increasingly out of reach. The walls of Troy stood firm, despite the years of onslaught. Many Greeks had perished, as had many Trojans, but the upper hand still lay with Troy, with its formidable walls.

It's almost surprising to look back and wonder why it took ten years for the Greeks to realize that if victory was to be theirs, they had to come up with a different strategy. A tactic they had yet to consider. That new strategy came in the form of a ploy, what history has recorded as the Trojan Horse. Historians differ as to who originally devised the idea but many credit Odysseus, that great and celebrated figure of the Odyssey.

It was Odysseus who recognized that without the assailing of the city walls, the war would continue in its current and fruitless path. And without victory, there would be no honor for the Greeks. It was this acknowledgment that caused him to devise a ruse, something that would hit at the heart of the Trojan fortress, as well as the one thing that gave the Trojans their greatest sense of security. *Those walls.* They had been the Greeks greatest barrier to victory.

The emblem of Troy was the horse. They were a horse-loving people. So that Trojan Horse served as a natural way of invoking the pride of the Trojans, while at the same time limiting their wariness. Under orders from Odysseus, the sculptor Epeius built a massive horse, which was left before the city as an offering to the gods, and as a memento to the Trojans for a war well fought. The hapless Trojans saw no signs of the Greek warships, for they had retreated just out of sight and were awaiting nightfall. Inside the great horse, thirty Greek warriors lay hidden, waiting for their plan to unfold.

This is where the story gets fascinating for me. Imagine the Trojans, peering from the safety of their walls, the sight of the battlefield before them. For the first time in a decade the plain lay empty. In the distance, a seascape finally free of enemy warships. A calm resulted that they had not experienced in some time. Before them stood a lone

9

wooden horse, massive and stately; an instantly recognizable gift. You can almost hear the excitement of those who first came upon the sight as they began to yell out to others. The news would have spread fast, reaching the ears of King Priam of Troy himself.

The ancient author Virgil describes the actual encounter of the Trojans with the Horse. A lone Greek soldier by the name of Sinon volunteered to stay behind and presented himself to the Trojan envoy. He convinces them that the Greeks have sailed off, leaving him behind and the Horse as well. The Horse, he tells them, is an offering to the goddess Athena, meant to atone for the Greeks' desecration of her temple at Troy, and to garner her favor as they sail again for home. Sinon even goes so far as to say that the Horse was built large enough to discourage the Trojans from taking it into the city, thus stealing the favor of Athena away from the Greeks.

But the scheme was not without its skeptics. There were two Trojans who saw through the ruse: a priest by the name of Laocoon, and Cassandra, the daughter of King Priam himself, who was considered the soothsayer of Troy. Both warned that the Horse was a trap and the fall of Troy would be imminent if they took it into the city. Even Helen of Troy is said to have raised concern over accepting this gift from the Greeks. One of the most quoted lines of the war comes from the warning by the priest Laocoon who said, "I fear Greeks, even those bearing gifts."

Despite the cries of warning, the pride of Troy was elevated, and the voices of those who saw the dangers were drowned out. The Horse was taken into the city and the rest as they say, is history. That evening, safely within the walls of Troy, and with most of its inhabitants either asleep or passed out from celebrating, the Greeks opened the gates to their waiting countrymen. The walls that held the enemy at bay for ten years were now consequential to the outcome. The city fell, ransacked and burned, and an era of warring came to an end.

One simple ploy and the Greeks were victorious. Walls that had previously protected a legendary city now became its greatest weakness because they trapped its citizens, rendering them helpless before a merciless enemy.

CHAPTER 1

Trojan Horses and the Task of Leadership

Management is doing things right; leadership is doing the right things. Peter Drucker

Hold yourself responsible for a higher standard than anybody expects of you. Never excuse yourself. Henry Ward Beecher

You are probably wondering what this has to do with a book on leadership? What can a war from the distant past possibly teach us about leadership in a hyper-connected and MBA saturated world? I believe the story of the Trojan Horse teaches us one of the most fundamental truths about leadership, one that can go unnoticed and even ignored, but has always been one of the key ingredients in every defeat, every failure, every loss, and every derailment.

Consider the walls of Troy again. For ten years they stood as the single greatest strength for the Trojans. From the perspective of the war, it was the one advantage the Trojans had over the Greeks. Yes, Troy had Hector, but he fell to Achilles (who by the way fell to Paris). Yes, they had a strong army, disciplined and resilient. But so did the Greeks. Troy had King Priam, strong and determined, but the Greeks had Agamemnon, fearless and equally determined. Each side had its heroes and its strengths, and each side proved their worth in the many years of fighting that ended in a stalemate.

Until that Horse! And that Horse targeted one thing and one thing alone: those walls and getting inside them. The greatest physical asset for the Trojans became their undoing. Though some warned of the ploy, their voices were left unheeded due to the pride of the Trojans who believed that the war had been won. They let down their guard and allowed the enemy into the one place they were safe: behind those walls. And once inside, the Greeks used those walls to their advantage.

For centuries, the Trojan War has stood as an illustration of military and strategic inventiveness. The Trojan Horse has particularly been cast as the star of the Greeks ploy and the decisive factor for tipping the scales in favor of the Greeks. But The Trojan Horse was far more than a prop, and far more than a diversion for hiding Greek warriors. Its real power lay elsewhere. Something far more insidious than a ruse that was nothing more than a sleight of hand.

I've alluded to the real genius behind the Trojan Horse already, and without it, the Horse would never have been successful. It's a variable that has played out in scores of scenarios throughout the scope of human history. We have all fallen prey to it at one time or another, sometimes with devastating results. And as the Trojans can attest, it brought a ten-year war to a disastrous end.

What the Trojan Horse so cleverly tapped into was the pride of the Trojans. Yes, there were other parts of the ploy that worked alongside the ruse, like the retreating of the Greek army away and out of sight. But at the heart of the plan was the hope of the Trojans sabotaging themselves. Their pride would be evoked to such degree that their cautiousness would dissolve, even to the point of disregarding the few voices that cried out in warning.

Until now, the enemy of Troy was easily identified. It had a name, a nationality, and a language of identity. It even had a geographic locale. For years, the label of Greek on the lips of a Trojan was synonymous with the term enemy. Now, that same enemy was using a more lethal tactic, one that comes in the shadows of the Trojans' very own hearts.

Up until that point, the leaders of Troy had been able to keep the Greeks at bay. Why would they not continue to trust their instincts? The great faith of the leaders is the faith they had in themselves. Why would their judgement fail, especially in light of the evidence before them? Did this not show the favor of the gods to the Trojans? Who could doubt the gods?

Strategic Captivity

Whether it's on a battlefield or in a boardroom, the greatest enemy lies within ourselves. It is often where the real battles are won or lost. We invest so much time and energy doing strategic analysis or comparative studies or market research that we can sometimes forget that no amount of preparation externally will compensate for dysfunctional failures internally.

I have spent years in leadership roles, first in business and then in pastoral ministry. I love the subject of leadership and believe it to be one of the most important roles in making any process better, any cause more worthy, any principle more valuable. Whether you are in a small context or a large one, competent leadership is often the defining difference. I have known incredible leaders, some of whom I have counted as friends and mentors and who have modeled it well. Unfortunately, I have also been subjected to leaders who were defined as leaders by title only.

I have been a keen observer of leaders. I have studied leadership principles and watched as the varying definitions and philosophies permeated the culture at large, even into the sacred realm of the church, whose leadership model is probably one of the best defined and demonstrated of all.[1]

From these years of observing and interacting with leaders,

some disturbing patterns emerge. Whenever a leader falls, we tend to instinctively look for culprits such as an addiction, an appetite, a lust, a character weakness, anything that can justify how a talented and gifted individual could be brought down. In some cases, the individual is so talented, is such a rising star, that we cannot imagine how a person with so much potential, so much talent, was not able to compensate for their weaknesses.

How often do we hear of CEOs who were geniuses in the boardroom but immoral in the bedroom. A gifted character actor on screen but a relational mess off screen. Or the gifted and inspiring communicator who could draw a crowd but lost their moral authority because of financial impropriety. I've noticed something else over the years. It doesn't matter what the arena is, whether business, government sector, non-profits, or church ministries, the pattern for derailment and self-sabotage are relatively consistent.

Most of us in hearing of these failures default to the common perception that it was a weakness that they could not control that ended up controlling them. We all struggle with appetites, and sometimes they do overwhelm and get the better of us. We certainly do not want to discount the role that our weaknesses play.

However, I believe that the way we treat these failures undermines a root cause of the failure in the first place. It isn't primarily our weaknesses that get us into trouble, but our strengths: the very character qualities that allow us to succeed, the very abilities that we become known for. The function that our strengths play as a culprit in self-sabotage has been neglected far too long. It's this point for which this book has been written. In sum:

- Our greatest strength can become our greatest weakness.
- Our greatest asset can become our greatest liability.
- Our greatest virtue can become our greatest vice.

I contend that more often than not it's our strengths, when they become vulnerable, that become the portal to a major fall. When we fail to acknowledge this, it potentially leaves us exposed to failure. Why? Because our strengths can be the least guarded part of our character. They are often left exposed and unprotected because we tend to think we are okay in those areas, because we've done well by them. They've gotten us to where we are today. Your strengths are why you succeed or why you've been put into a prominent leadership role. It's those very characteristics that cause you to be admired, followed, and even respected. Yet time after time, gifted people, with incredible strengths and intelligence, are making dumb mistakes that cost them dearly. And for many of these leaders, a lifetime of trust, integrity, and work becomes undermined.

In truth, our strengths can become the vehicle for self-sabotage; and the greater the capacity of our strengths, the greater the capacity for sabotaging those strengths. We can become blinded by the very characteristics that have made us a leader. Our strengths can become overblown or overused to such degree that their usefulness becomes nullified. This is one of the ways our strengths can become our weakness.

I believe there is a second way. We can allow a weakness or a character flaw to debilitate our strengths to the point that they are rendered useless. Either way, our effectiveness has been compromised. And what really stings is this. It only takes a minor weakness to topple a major strength.

These have grave implications for leaders. What makes us gifted to lead is in fact our greatest potential for failure. Though we have identified two possibilities concerning our strengths, it only takes one to bring us crashing down. It doesn't matter whether a strength we have has made us successful and thereby created in us a lack of humility that evokes pride, or that a particular fear debilitates us from making a decision at a key moment; our ability to lead effectively has been compromised.

When I looked up Trojan Horse on Wikipedia I was amused to read, "Metaphorically, a 'Trojan Horse' has come to mean any trick or stratagem that causes a target to invite a foe into a securely protected bastion or space." No wonder it's a term that has been adopted by the computer industry.

Unlike the software definition above, our personal strengths are not necessarily protected space. Likely due to our lack of recognizing their vulnerability. Hence their potential as a target to be exploited. In the pages that follow we're going to unveil the Trojan Horse of leadership and discover the one thing that can undermine us and cause us to fail; the one thing that allows us to lower our guard and invite an enemy in.

Before going any further I want to clarify what we consider to be the definition of a strength. It's not necessarily what you are good at or even that thing at which you are most accomplished. There are many things in life that we can do well, but give us little satisfaction or sense of accomplishment. A true strength is whatever you are good at that gives you energy, a sense of purpose, and that naturally motivates and inspires you. It is something that others see in you and want to emulate or follow. It won't always come easily but it will satisfy you in ways nothing else can.

I would contend a further point given as part of that definition. A true strength won't just give you personal satisfaction, but others will recognize it as a true strength of yours as well. As a leader, they will see your strengths as inspiring and worth developing in you. Further, it would be one of the key reasons people follow you, and maybe even copy your values and strengths. At the very least, when asked what makes you a good leader, your strengths will be the first things that come to mind.

Those closest will know when you are operating in the area of your strengths. Most tend to light up, or give off a sense of urgency or excitement that is palpable to those around them. As we will see in the pages that follow, this can be both a good and wondrous thing, but can also become a potential for derailment if we are not careful. The very virtue that frames our good side can also lead us into a corresponding vice.

The Walls we Construct

We've all heard people say, "I should have known better," or, "I can't believe I did that." In my own life, my greatest failures have come by way of my greatest strengths. I knew at the time that I was allowing something into my life that could have serious repercussions. But even with the warnings going off inside, as well as members of my family stating their concern, I still went ahead. Why? Because I didn't believe that I could fall in that one area. Because it had served me flawlessly for years. I knew what I was doing and I had navigated these waters before without any harm. Boy was I wrong! I thought the walls were strong enough, and indeed they were. I just didn't see my Trojan Horse until it was too late, and the enemy was already inside.

I've become convinced of this from another source as well. Since 1996 I have had the privilege of teaching at a bible college and seminary, primarily in the books of the Old Testament. Over the years of teaching these courses, I noticed this same truth emerging from the pages of Scripture. Many of our most beloved biblical characters suffered from this same problem. Many of them failed God with their strengths, the very characteristics that defined them and the very virtues we know them for.

I suppose the easiest route would have been to tackle a character study of the lives of a select group of CEOs or politicians who have fallen, which would have had some benefit to the topic at hand.

However, the biblical characters are paragons of faith and virtue. They are saints, whose stories illuminate what happens when one entrusts themselves wholly into the hands of God. Yet despite their venerated status, they were human. And that is the wonder of the Bible. It doesn't mask this humanness or attempt to downplay it. It portrays the people in its pages in all their rawness, both good and bad. It's an honest book revealing a gracious God who interacts with His creation, despite our tendency to stray.

The point is not to disparage the biblical characters that we will look at, but to learn valuable lessons about their struggles, especially in the context of leadership. Many of these men and women who grace the pages of Scripture stood above the crowd, often leading with great faith in uncertain times. Yet in many of their stories, there are those moments when things go wrong, even fail miserably.

For example, Moses was a man who talked face to face with God, a man known for his meekness and his faithful adherence to the laws entrusted to him by the Lord. A man who defied a Pharaoh and led a people from exile into the Promised Land. Yet, for all of Moses' accomplishments, he was prohibited from entering the land himself. Why? How could this happen to a giant of the faith? It essentially came down to one unfortunate incident. Moses, the man who was known for his reverence for God, is not allowed to enter the Land of Promise because of one momentary lapse of irreverence. Imagine that.

And what about a man like Solomon. He is noted for being one of the wisest men in the entire Bible. Yet despite this accolade, Solomon did some of the most foolish things conceivable. Especially in light of what God had warned him not to do. He acted in direct defiance of God. That doesn't strike me as very wise. What happened or what changed to cause Solomon, this wise man, to end up so badly?

There are great lessons to be learned from these stories, not just for leadership, but for life in general. Whether its peer to peer relationships, or a boss over employees, recognizing the potential for a Trojan Horse is a giant step towards guarding an area that can have serious consequences. We do this not just for ourselves, but for those who care about us too; those loved ones who are hurt by the very thing they in all likelihood admire and love us for.

And the concern for leadership is warranted in another significant way. The current leadership climate advocates for focusing on our strengths and ignoring our weaknesses. In other words, play to your strengths and your natural God-given abilities. After all, isn't that how God wired you? Isn't that the path to success and fulfilling what God put you on this earth for? I actually endorse these principles wholeheartedly, but with one caveat: Make a commitment to guard yourself from the potential your strengths have to derail you. I'm not stating for a minute that every strength we have is going to undermine us, or that a failure in this regard will permanently disqualify us from leadership altogether. In fact, many great leaders have rebounded from terrible failures. But the reality is this: The very strengths we depend upon, left unguarded and unprotected, can lead us into harm's way.

As we learned in the story of the Trojan War, the horse was simply a means of gaining entrance into the stronghold of Troy. It was the delivery system for getting Greek warriors behind the city walls. The Trojans, believing that the war was over, allowed their defenses to be compromised by their own pride. To borrow another metaphor from the war, it became their Achilles heel.

Whether we are aware of it or not, our strengths can become undermined in a similar way. Our Trojan Horse could be a fear, a moral compulsion, or any number of character flaws. Because we are human, we are composed of abilities and frailties as part of our natural make-up. Yet rarely do we succeed at anything because of our weaknesses, even though they are what keep counsellors and psychotherapists in business. Our strengths are what make us successful, marketable, and even admired.

Doesn't it make sense that we should not just celebrate and maximize our strengths, but guard them as well? Or at least make an attempt to understand how our strengths can contribute to the potential of self-sabotage? Regardless of the size or nature of the organization or people you lead, your ability to accomplish what has been entrusted to you lies solely in the investment you make in developing your character. It is without a doubt the single greatest investment you can make to guard yourself from the potential of self-destructing.

In his book, *How the Mighty Fall*, Jim Collins researched how even great companies can fall and makes this observation:

> Every institution is vulnerable, no matter how great. No matter how much you've achieved, no matter how far you've gone, no matter how much power you've garnered, you are vulnerable to decline. There is no law of nature that the most powerful will inevitably remain on top. Anyone can fall and most eventually do.[2]

What is true of the corporate world can also be true of the individual. We all have a potential vulnerability that can leave us exposed to derailment, but rarely do we see our strengths as a vulnerability. We feel immune to the probability of self-sabotage because the warning signs are rarely loud enough to be heard. They often come from somewhere outside of ourselves and may even come from a place that we would consider unimportant, irrelevant, or non-threatening.

No leader ever fails just himself or herself. There is always collateral damage. Those who are affected in the wake of a fall are often the closest to the leader; the ones who have the most invested and the ones who have the most to lose.

As an advocate for leadership, I believe God has gifted certain individuals to carry the leadership mantle. Due my burden for leaders, and the important role they play in the world around us, I hope this book will help you guard what is likely your greatest asset so it doesn't become your greatest liability. Its aim is to protect you from a potential Trojan Horse in your life and leadership and in the pages that follow, we will unpack the lives of biblical characters who failed at their strengths and what we can learn from them. Not only as an academic exercise, but also as a means by which we can grow in our own awareness and leadership.

A leader's lack of self-awareness can become the leader's greatest barrier. What is true about a Trojan Horse is that they are often self-inflicted; and anytime you allow something to diminish your capacity to lead from your strengths it undermines your ability to lead well, or to lead at all.

The more we understand our strengths and the more we comprehend the delicate balance of leading from those strengths, the more aware we become of the possibility for self-sabotage. So many great leaders who have gone before have fallen, so what would make us think we are impervious to the same plight? What has been demonstrated time and again is that an unguarded strength is potentially more dangerous than a guarded weakness.

The matter of a leader's self-awareness is important, not only in acknowledging the potential character risks but also how context plays a vital role as well. A topic we will be looking at in a later chapter. For now I want to state this: The primary strengths that are intrinsic in a leader usually apply to certain contexts. Those same strengths, when utilized outside of them, typically lead to some kind of dysfunction, or even disaster.

If you are a conscientious leader, wouldn't you appreciate knowing the potential hazards? The hope is that this book will assist you in guarding your greatest assets-your strengths-and by doing so, make you a more productive and effective leader. Because for every leader that brings their best, the world becomes a better place.

CHAPTER 2

Where No Man Has Gone Before

And so it happened just as the Scriptures say: "Abraham believed God, and God counted him as righteous because of his faith." He was even called the friend of God. (James 2:23)

Abraham, you simply cannot discuss the giants of faith without him. He epitomizes what it means to be a person committed to God. He is the prototype of faith. Three of the world's religions claim him as their spiritual father. After all, he is the one whom God told to move from the comforts of his homeland, uproot family and belongings, and forge a way westward. Did I mention that God never gave him a specific destination except for the general direction of the land of Canaan? And still, despite the seeming incongruity of God's request, he went.

In Genesis 12:1, God instructs Abraham to pack up and go to a land that God is going to show him. We are never privy to the roadmap or specifically the directions that God presented him with. But from the outset, Abraham had to trust God for the direction of his travels. Granted, the impulse to move out was footnoted by a promise that God would make Abraham great, his progeny great, and would bless the entire world through him. Whoever became a friend of Abraham's would find favor with God, but whoever became his enemy would have God to deal with.

That's quite a promise attached to the prodding to leave, but prior to chapter 12 we have no hint of Abraham having any kind of familiarity or relationship with God. In fact, Abraham, without any apparent prior experience with God, had to trust that what God was saying to him would in fact materialize. Remember, Abraham lived in a region fraught with gods of all kinds, and he would have been familiar with all the rituals meant for garnering the favor, or appeasing the anger, of the gods. It was traditionally a one-way relationship whereby a sacrifice is made, and then the hopeful expectation that whatever god you were attempting to please, would accept your sacrifice and grant your request.

But here Abraham is promised much more. It's not just a year of good crops, or good health, or even vast personal wealth. God's promise to Abraham contains much more. All without a hint of a history between God and Abraham to validate it. Besides, had Abraham ever been to Canaan prior to this? What was it like? What had he heard? Did he know anyone from that region from whom he had heard stories? Even so, the move to a new land, one which entails uprooting family and all possessions, would be fraught with anxiety in this day and age, let alone the historical period in which Abraham lived .

Imagine for a moment that you have come home and told your wife that God has spoken to you, telling you to pack up your family and move. What kind of response do you suppose you would initially receive? I'd imagine some form of laughter would be a safe bet. At worst you would get one of those looks that you may get from time to time when your wife thinks you've been in the sun too long. And it wouldn't stop there. After the laughter subsides and some form of decorum is regained imagine the obvious question she's been dying to ask: "Where does God say we should move too?"

Can you feel it? That lump in your throat when you realize that what you're about to say is definitely going to make her think you've totally lost it. Here it comes: "God just said that He will show me, that it's in that general direction." It's at that moment that you realize that you've lifted your arm and pointed towards the west wall of your house, the one where just last week you remodeled and painted because this is where you were planning to live until the kids finished school. How quickly do you suppose the family would be packing boxes and loading up the u-haul?

I think you get the idea. Abraham, from the outset, had to trust God. And it's much more than a casual hopefulness that things will work out. Throughout the life of Abraham, God is prompting him to trust Him further. And for most of their time together the one thing that Abraham asks God for, the one thing that is weighing on Abraham's heart, is his desire to have a son.

It's as if there are two separate conversations going on. God is talking to Abraham about making his name great, and to make a nation from him and to bless the world through him, while through it all, Abraham just wants a son. An heir that will carry on the family name and legacy, never mind all this talk of a multitude. It's not until Abraham is 100 years old that the son that God promised him finally comes. But that is getting ahead of ourselves.

The Stage is Set

There are two little stories pertaining to the life of Abraham that are found in Genesis – and both of them are very similar. The fact that this scene is played out twice in the life of Abraham is remarkable. One is found in Genesis 12:10-20 and the second is found in Genesis 20:1-20. In both stories, Abraham instructs his wife Sarah to tell everyone that she is his sister, because Sarah is very beautiful and Abraham fears that the locals will kill him if they find out he's really her husband. For whatever reason, real or not, Abraham is concerned for his own safety. And the fact that Sarah is beautiful, raises the validity of Abraham's anxiety.

The first story of Genesis 12 takes place in Egypt and the second story is the one we are going to look a bit closer at. That's the one found in Genesis 20—let me frame the story a bit for you here. Abraham has traveled into the region of Gerar—known more commonly as the land of the Philistines. And again, as in the first story of Genesis 12 in Egypt, he once again tells everyone that Sarah his wife is his sister.

Sarah's beauty soon gains the attention of the king of that region, a man by the name of Abimelech, who takes her into his harem. For the record, Sarah is probably ninety years old at this time, proving that beauty doesn't just reside with the young.

The scene is now set. It doesn't take long before Abimelech senses that something is wrong. In fact, the warning comes the very first night. Let's take a look at the story as it unfolds in Genesis 20.

But that night God came to Abimelech in a dream and told him, "You are a dead man, for that woman you have taken is already married!" But Abimelech had not slept with her yet, so he said, "Lord, will you destroy an innocent nation? Didn't Abraham tell me, 'She is my sister?' And she herself said, 'Yes, he is my brother.' I acted in complete innocence! My hands are clean." In the dream God responded, "Yes, I know you are innocent. That's why I kept you from sinning against me, and why I did not let you touch her. Now return the woman to her husband, and he will pray for you, for he is a prophet. Then you will live. But if you don't return her to him, you can be sure that you and all your people will die." (Genesis 20:3-7)

One of the significant things to note is that in that culture, to abduct another man's wife was to destroy that man's home. That is one of the reasons that over the course of history, the targeting of women by an invading force was a tactical move for demoralizing those they wanted to conquer.

Yet in this case, the taking of Sarah by Abimelech is not for those reasons. All sexual innuendos aside, Abimelech, upon hearing God's indictment of his actions defends himself as having acted in innocence. In fact, both Abraham and Sarah are complicit in the ruse. Both participated in the lie as a means of protection. But protection from what? From whom?

When we stand back and observe the story objectively we cannot help but acknowledge that the person who demonstrates the most integrity is Abimelech. From the moment that God reveals what is going on the king appeals to God's sense of justice. That if he is an innocent man and if God is just, then He would do no harm to him for something of which he had no knowledge. But God's message to the king is very clear: Return her or else!

The story continues with Abimelech getting up the very next morning and calling his servants together. Upon telling them what happened, verse 8 records that they were all terrified. This is a significant thing to note. Abimelech could have avoided the embarrassment of being tricked and just have returned Sarah to Abraham quietly. Instead, he is willing to admit publicly that he has been duped. Once again, the integrity of Abimelech and even his servants is pictured in stark contrast to that of Abraham and Sarah. The text continues in verse 9 with Abimelech confronting Abraham and the interaction is quite revealing:

Then Abimelech called for Abraham. "What have you done to us?" he demanded. "What crime have I committed that deserves treatment like this, making me and my kingdom guilty of this great sin? No one should ever do what you have done! Whatever possessed you to do such a thing?" Abraham replied, "I thought, 'This is a godless place. They will want my wife and will kill me to get her.' And she really is my sister, for we both have the same father, but different mothers. And I married her. When God called me to leave my father's home and to travel from place to place, I told her, 'Do me a favor. Wherever we go, tell the people that I am your brother.'" (Genesis 20:9-13)

When the king asks for the reasons for Abraham's lie he responds with two assumptions. He assumed it was a godless place and that they would kill him for his wife. Now these assumptions have been generated by Abraham because of one primary reason. Fear. Notice the last sentence in the passage. From the very beginning of their travels, Abraham has been portraying Sarah as his sister. It has been a pattern from the beginning, a fabrication of the reality of their relationship. Even though Sarah is Abraham's half-sister, this half-truth doesn't warrant the deception, nor make Abraham's actions legitimate. And in the case of this particular story, it is a deception fueled by a fear that is further fueled by an assumption. That is a powerful combination, and one that undermines the character of a man who is renowned for his faith. A faith that from the beginning was characterized by trust.

The Havoc Unleashed

Fear is a powerful thing and in no way are we to minimize the potential danger that may have existed for Abraham and Sarah. The possibility of what he feared was not unwarranted. Still, because of that fear, Abraham assumed something that caused him to act callously and put Sarah in harm's way. Especially when the writer of the story goes out of his way to show Abimelech as a God-fearing king. One who exemplifies honorable character above that of Abraham. As a result of Abraham's fear, he was unable to ascertain the situation around him with any kind of clarity. Fear has a way of clouding our judgement.

The disparity between Abraham and Abimelech is striking. The fear that fueled Abraham's assumptions also diminished his character when contrasted with Abimelech, who, as king, could have protected himself from ridicule and disposed of the matter quietly. Instead, he does not allow his position or his power to negate his character when it comes to the taking of Sarah. He openly exposes not only the ruse, but the inappropriateness of taking another's wife. Thereby bringing to the forefront the complicity of Abraham and Sarah in portraying themselves as something they were not, regardless if it was partially true. It is Abimelech throughout this short narrative interlude who believes and trusts God at his word, not Abraham.

Not only is Abimelech's character shown by the way he is morally repulsed by the situation, but he also compensates Abraham materially. He showers the patriarch with livestock, slaves, silver, and an offer to live wherever he chooses. Actions that in that culture amounts to a formal apology. Who is the one standing on higher ground?

The seriousness of the situation was such that God had closed the womb of every woman in Abimelech's household. If Abraham was unaware of the gravity of his deception, Abimelech was not. Surely God was well aware of the implications. Here, on two occasions (Genesis 12 and 20), Abraham jeopardizes the promise of God to give Abraham an heir through Sarah by literally allowing other men to take her. The motives for such actions were known all too well at the time.

There is an interesting postlude to the story of Abraham and Abimelech. In the closing verses we read these words:

Then Abraham prayed to God, and God healed Abimelech, his wife, and his female servants, so they could have children. For the Lord had caused all the women to be infertile because of what happened with Abraham's wife, Sarah. (Genesis 20:17-18)

Notice the opening phrase, "Then Abraham prayed to God."

Why would Abraham have to go through the motion of praying? God even told Abimelech earlier in the story that Abraham would pray for him. Throughout the entire ordeal, God has been intimately involved and even intervened in order to protect Sarah, so why put the onus on Abraham to pray? God could easily have brought resolution to the events without the action of Abraham's prayer.

God takes this opportunity to teach Abraham some important truths, primarily what happens when fear and faith collide. Fear has a way of disconnecting us from God, of causing us to rationalize our fear by attempting to control the circumstances around us. For Abraham, his fear, no matter how much he could justify it, caused him to rely on deception rather than on God. Abraham found comfort in the deception, hoping that it would protect him from what he perceived as potential threats to his well-being.

The prayer is God's object lesson to Abraham. God, all powerful, all knowing, doesn't lift a finger until Abraham surrenders in prayer. A prayer that reminds him of his need to trust God with the outcome, not his fear. That the indiscretions of the patriarch are not ignored and that God will demand that things are made right. Deception always comes with consequences regardless of our tendency to rationalize it.

Abraham, distracted by his fear, has threatened everything around him. His faith, Sarah's life, Abimelech's entire household and kingdom, God's reputation and ultimately His plan of blessing Sarah with a child is put in jeopardy. That is a lot of collateral damage generated by one man's fear.

God's request of Abraham to pray is that moment when Abraham must acknowledge his Trojan Horse. The subtle nature of fear to undermine an otherwise obedient servant of God. Not only for the potential of what it can do to him directly, but how it can also hurt those around him. Look at what it cost Abimelech. He lavished Abraham with gifts in order to compensate for any wrong he may have done. The reputation of both men were threatened by the incident and in the ancient near east, the loss of a person's word placed their character in peril. Not an attractive option for a king. The wrong way to view this story is to say that Abraham actually gained materially from his deception. Rather we should consider what the lie cost Abimelech.

God is also aware of another truth. Failure is often an opportunity to learn some of life's greatest lessons. One of the key reasons for God taking the time to nurture Abraham through his failure is to take every advantage possible to impart to him the lesson of trust. God would not allow Abraham to walk away and not learn from it. How often do we fully grasp the lessons of failure, rather than treat them as dead ends with nothing worth remembering? In truth, our most profound lessons come through our most pronounced failures.

It is in this moment that Abraham comes full faced into the reality of his potential to fail, while at the same time learning afresh the nature of the God he serves. The chasm is wide, yet it is here at this juncture where we learn the lessons of true dependency, faith, and trust.

How real do you think Abraham's faith would have been to Abimelech and the people of his court? A man who had demonstrated trust in God by leaving his homeland to wander where God led him could not have looked all that trusting of the God he claimed to follow. Without the direct intervention of God, the outcome of the story would have been much different.

In Chapter 15 of Genesis, God appears in a vision to Abraham and gives him these words: "Do not be afraid, Abram, for I will protect you, and your reward will be great." It seems that God was fully cognizant of the potential for Abraham to fear. What is interesting about this particular passage is that it is somewhat difficult contextually to understand why God is saying this in the first place. The best that can be deduced is that Abraham is fretting over his desire to have an heir. God's assurance of protection and reward are mitigated by the admonition of "Do not be afraid," which is one of the most common phrases in the entire Bible.

What do we say about a giant of the faith who has a tendency to deceive in moments when fear is aroused? For Abraham, fear was his Trojan Horse. Fear, whether real or imagined, has a way of diluting faith. It can take a giant like Abraham, who in many ways demonstrated incredible faith, and cause him to doubt in other areas that undermine an otherwise faithful and trusting servant of God. Fear drove Abraham to lie in order to protect himself rather than trust God. The faith of Abraham capitulated to fear. In doing so, he put Sarah at risk but more importantly, God's plan at risk. It took direct intervention by God to protect the promise that He had made, all of which was being threatened by the actions of Abraham.

Here We Go Again

We have looked at length at Abraham's indiscretion with Abimelech in Genesis 20 and stated that it mimics an earlier one in Genesis 12 with another powerful man, the Pharaoh of Egypt. But these are not the only instances of Abraham struggling with fear. In between these two stories, we read of Abraham fathering a child outside of God's stated intention and purpose.

In Chapter 16, Sarah, fearing that God had forgotten His promise, suggests to Abraham that he father a child through her servant Hagar. Abraham, having already voiced his desire for an heir, and also fearing that God had forgotten them, takes the matter into his own hands and willingly agrees. The union produces a son, Ishmael, and a cycle of inter-personal conflict begins.

It generates conflict between Sarah and Hagar, Sarah and Abraham, God and Sarah, God and Abraham, Ishmael and Sarah, and eventually, Ishmael and Isaac, who was the heir that God had originally intended all along. Conflict initiated by Abraham's fear that he would die with no one to carry on the family legacy despite God's promise to the contrary.

We often hear how our actions have consequences. What is true today was true in Abraham's time. The moments of fear that pushed the patriarch to deception become a pattern in his descendants. Abraham's son Isaac mimics his parents in Genesis 26. Oddly enough, the place is Gerar and the name of the king, Abimelech. It is likely that by this time the king is either a son or grandson of the earlier king by the same name but the circumstances are identical. This time Isaac, whose wife Rebekah was also described as beautiful, tells the men of Gerar that she is his sister. What was a half-truth for Abraham is an outright lie for Isaac.

But it doesn't end there. The sons of Isaac and Rebekah, Jacob and Esau, had their own moments fraught with conflict. Encouraged by his mother, Jacob devises a plan which openly deceives his father and usurps the birthright from his brother Esau. The fracture caused by this deception is felt for years and shows up again in the next generation by way of Jacobs' sons. They were the ones who conspired against their own brother Joseph whom they shipped off as a slave to Egypt, while lying to their father that he was killed by a wild animal.

What needs to be stressed at this juncture is this: A major theme in Genesis is sin, and one of the ways it is graphically illustrated is in humanity's propensity to lie and deceive. Even if it is seen in those we would otherwise consider idyllic examples of godly saints. After-all, does it not give us a more realistic picture of the human dilemma we all struggle with? Is it not true that deception has a way of preventing blessing and invoking consequences?

And I do not mean to write the epitaph of Abraham and his descendants as liars. To characterize an entire individual's life by their indiscretions would be unfair. However, it does demonstrate the potential that something like fear can have in undermining an otherwise strong characteristic like faith and turning it into a liability. Without the direct revelation and confirmation of God about who Abraham was, his strength of faith would have been suspect to those around him. It may have been seen as part of the overall ruse itself.

In fact, when we read the entire account of Abraham there is a progression. By the time of Abraham's ultimate test in Chapter 22, his faith and trust in God is unwavering. Though Abraham has stumbled, he has learned from those previous lessons well. From the outset of their relationship Abraham has asked God for only one thing, a son. And when the appointed heir arrives, God tests the faith of Abraham by asking him to sacrifice the one thing he's ever really wanted. There is no greater demand that God can make on Abraham but for the very thing the patriarch has asked for all along.

Our modern sensibilities cannot fathom the details of such a story. But the major lesson for us at this juncture of Abraham's life is his unwavering faith in God, regardless of how uncomfortable we are with the context. Besides, the opening verses of Chapter 22 imply that this was a test of Abraham's faith and God was not going to let anything happen to Isaac. It may be reasonable to assert that if Abraham was to become the father of all believers, then the degree and extent of his faithfulness would likely need to be tested the most.

Why include the stories of Abraham's shortcomings at all? Do they not diminish our view of Abraham, if not discount his character as a man of faith? My personal view is that this is what makes the Bible so timely, even in today's tech-savvy, hyper-connected world. It is what confirms in my mind the authenticity of its stories and the message that is intrinsic in its pages. What makes us human hasn't fundamentally changed throughout the centuries. God has a way of taking human frailty and weakness, and accomplishing His plan in spite of us. The same is true for our strengths, because our strengths tend to distance us from the need for God. Either way, God has a way of coming out on top.

If fear has the potential to undermine someone like Abraham, a man renowned for his allegiance to God, what warning does it give us? Here is a historical figure whose legacy is faith and trust in the one God, at a time when the world of gods and deities is overcrowded. To commit to one and one alone was in itself a remarkable submission on the part of Abraham. Yet, despite his legacy, we find a person who at times, acted in ways that belie his reputation as a man of profound faith. In those few moments, fear overtook his faith and prompted him to act in direct opposition to it.

CHAPTER 3

The Trojan Horse of Fear

"You gain strength, courage, and confidence by every experience in which you stop to look fear in the face. You are able to say to yourself, 'I lived through this horror. I can take the next thing that comes along.' The danger lies in refusing to face the fear, in not daring to come to grips with it." Eleanor Roosevelt

When I was growing up there was a famous daredevil named Evel Knievel. He came to prominence by jumping over rows of vehicles with his motorcycle, his longest being a jump of 14 buses. He soon graduated to jumping canyons with rocket powered sky-cycles and even set his sights on vaulting the Grand Canyon, even though the US Government never gave him permission. He's recorded to have broken over 400 bones and holds a place in the Guinness Book of World Records for "Most Bones Broken in a Lifetime." One of his sons, Robbie, followed in his father's daredevil footsteps.

One of the most memorable TV commercials from my youth involved Evel and his son Robbie sitting in a garage surrounded by their many motorcycles and stuntmen paraphernalia. Both were boasting in their accomplishments and comparing the number of scars and broken bones they had earned in their careers as stuntmen. It was pure macho driven adrenaline. For a few brief moments we were invited into the world of extreme stunts and dangerous escapism few of us could imagine. Suddenly, into this testosterone rich environment appears a common household spider and the two men, known for their fearlessness become whimpering cowards. What was a time of courageous gloating turns into a chaotic scramble by both men to get out as fast as they can. In the closing moments of the commercial you can hear Evel yell out, "Go get your mother!"

Consider for a moment if their fear of spiders was in any way that paralyzing. What effect would that fear have on their ability to jump if during one of their attempts they spied a tarantula on the ramp? Imagine being at full throttle, barreling toward the onramp that will launch you and your cycle into the air and over rows of cars, only to suddenly catch sight of this slow moving multi-legged hairy creature taking its sweet time on the very trajectory you are heading?

Not sure if this would be true of you, but I know if it was me, I would lose all attention to critical details. The kind of focus that would be needed for such a feat would be totally compromised. Bike speed, alignment with the ramp, posture and positioning, flight dynamics, landing protocol, all of it would now become secondary because that furry thing on the ramp has captured my attention. My options are few now. I can power through and hope for the best, even though it won't be an ideal effort, or I can miss the ramp altogether and hopefully be able to compose myself to try again. That is the kind of impact fear can have on our leadership. It can debilitate us from performing the very thing we're best at, even known for.

To this day I cannot remember what product or service was being advertised, and I cannot find any hint of it on the internet today, but I've always remembered the ad because of its impact. The commercial would have been lost from my collective memory years ago had the contrasts not been so strong. Two men, famous for their ability to face dangerous and perilous stunts, brought low by a common household spider. No one, having walked into that garage in the midst of their meltdown, would have believed them to be world renowned daredevils. In fact, the suggestion of such a thing, at the very least, would have been met with skepticism if not outright doubt.

A Fear by Any Other Name

The potential effect fear can have in your life cannot be overstated. It can create a climate of chaos in an otherwise normal environment. Now some of you will object to the previous story and say we are talking about a phobia, specifically arachnophobia, the fear of spiders. That may be true, but regardless of how we identify the feeling, whether a full-blown phobia or a nagging anxiety, they all share the common potential of becoming a Trojan Horse in your life. It is just the degree of their effects. Whether overt like a phobia or a more subtle fear, they all have the potential to derail us in some way.

As a pastor I'm introduced to people's fears all the time. It is therefore no surprise to me that the most repeated command in the Bible is "Do not fear!" It is undoubtedly one of our greatest human frailties and I would even venture to say it is one of the distinct characteristics that every human shares. Whenever someone confides in me about a tension in his or her life, invariably a fear surfaces.

In virtually every conversation there is a tacit acknowledgement that fear has diminished their ability to live life to it's fullest. There is this sense of unrealized potential, a dream that was thwarted, a hope that was dashed, a preferred future that was aborted. All due to fear fostering in them a posture that never allowed them to take even the first step forward.

I'm sure what I am about to say next is one of the most tired anxieties the travel industry has heard, but because it is shared by so many we should not discount its validity. Though I love to travel, getting on an airplane is a necessary evil. I can't tell you the number of times I've allowed the anxiety of getting on a plane to diminish the excitement of the destination.

Though I've gotten used to it I cannot shake the uncomfortable feeling I get whenever I board an airplane. I've even dreamed of the day when technology will allow us to go from destination to destination simply by being transported in true Star Trek fashion. Even though transporter technology demands taking apart your molecular structure and reconfiguring it in a different location, perhaps thousands of miles away, in some twisted way I'm more comfortable with that than hanging some thirty-thousand feet in the air. Okay, I never said that fear was rational.

Fear can manifest itself in a number of ways. Fear of conflict, fear of failure, fear of rejection, even fear of success. In the lives of most leaders there is a tendency to compensate in the area of their greatest fear. It can make itself evident in the way a leader overcompensates to the detriment of their strengths. If you struggle with self-worth you may overcompensate with self-promotion, even though you may be incredibly gifted at relationship building.

I have a dear friend who is incredibly likeable, everyone wants to be his friend and he has the ability to make anyone feel comfortable. He soaks in the attention he receives from those around him. He makes it look so easy and natural, yet personally, he struggles with his value and self-worth. Because that fear is part of him, he tends to make many acquaintances but few real friends. Most of the relationships in his life are superficial. And since he rarely allows himself to invest deeply in others, his self-worth also suffers, because it's rarely confirmed or affirmed in a way that only true friends could.

Fighting Back

A Trojan Horse is a delivery system. Like the one that delivered a Greek army into the heart of Troy, a leader's potential for derailment can be accelerated by whatever they allow to weaken them. And one of the most potent Trojan Horses is fear. Even though there are moments and circumstances where fear is legitimate, for the most part, our fear is often self-imposed. It can create in us a cycle of self-victimization. It becomes a boundary marker and without a conscious attempt to overcome that fear, or even to acknowledge the limitations it places on us, our leadership will be governed by the boundaries that it sets.

There are countless leadership books that advocate for actively developing your strengths. Like any artistic endeavor, leadership is a craft you can hone and improve, but few of these resources talk in terms of a fear inventory as a way of developing your leadership strengths. That is not to diminish the value of focused commitment to strength development, but to ignore the potential limitations that something like fear can have is short sighted.

Tim Irwin has studied and written on prominent CEO's who led multi-million dollar corporations but ended in career derailment. In his analysis, he states five common themes to every failure he investigated. One of his five is relevant to our discussion: "Derailment is not inevitable, but without attention to development, it is probable.[1]"

So those things that cause us to fear or well up with anxiety are not to be disregarded. But managing them is equally daunting. Fear has a way of clouding our judgement. Those moments when our fears are most predominant are the moments when clarity is difficult. A fog descends that can leave us incapacitated, so much so that even simple decisions become laborious. Even those decisions that in any other environment or context would have been dispensed with ease.

Collins, while researching why certain companies fall, recognized a pattern that exists when fear is allowed to dominate. He writes:

When we find ourselves in trouble, when we find ourselves falling, our survival instinct-our fear-can evoke lurching, reactive behavior absolutely contrary to survival. The very moment when we need to take calm deliberate action, we run the risk of doing the exact opposite and bringing about the very outcome we most fear[2].

Another study centered on the potential causes that limit innovation in an organization. It cited fear as the greatest obstacle. The study claimed that only 3% of employees surveyed considered themselves "fearless." Their findings placed fear as a major limitation, if not the predominant one. So, what are employees afraid of? Here is what the survey uncovered:[3]

- Fear of making a mistake topped the list (cited by 30%)
- Fear of getting fired. In fact, not only the fear of getting fired outright, but the fear of appearing less dedicated or vital if they actually take earned vacation days is a big issue in a slow economy. The data shows employees left an average of 11 vacation days untaken in 2011.
- Fear of dealing with difficult customers or clients
- Fear of conflict with a manager
- Fear of speaking in front of a group
- Fear of disagreements with co-workers

According to the authors, Morrison and Milliken, a fearful environment creates organizational fear in which employees end up whispering behind closed doors. Therefore, an organization which may pride itself on its employees lack of opposition to direction or decisions, may in fact have created such a culture of fear, that no employee would dare speak against the status-quo.

As Morrison and Milliken conclude, the most effective means of diffusing a culture of fear is by encouraging open communication. In their assessment, this one strategic change would provide the type of working relationship that would foster greater innovation and greater employee satisfaction.

In pondering the results of this survey and the conclusions of the authors, I wondered about the type of employer needed in order to allow such an openness to exist. Consider this. If the boss has any insecurity whatsoever, then his greatest fears would likely be realized in such a scenario. Imagine the people who work for you having the freedom to question or provide input. Most of your insecurities would be directly exposed and for anyone less than open about them it would not be an attractive proposition. Though this is the optimal scenario for creating highly effective teams, the degree in which the team struggles with individual's fears could render them unable to produce to their full potential.

I remember one of the more interesting references I've ever received. We were hiring for a new ministry position. The job description had been written for some time ago but was contingent on finding the right person. I had it clearly in mind the type of person we were looking for and it was almost two years before the right person with the right characteristics and personality mix showed up. I knew we had found who we needed.

I called one of their references and near the end of the call the person asked me a question that took me by surprise. They asked me if I was a secure person. A little stunned by the sudden query I stammered an answer something like, "I think so!" Their reason for asking the question was something I will never forget. The person we were looking to hire was so likeable, that if I had any insecurities in that regard then at some point their popularity would become an aggravation for me. And they did not want me to hire them if the eventual outcome was a confrontation between an insecure employer fearful of an employee who had more fans than he did.

I have to admit that after the call I took some time to reflect on what I heard. Would I be upset, even to the degree of plotting their termination if they became the darling of the organization? I can still remember asking myself if that scenario was even plausible? After some personal reflection I resolved that my insecurities lay in other areas so we went ahead with the hire. Suffice it to say that he became everything we were looking for in an employee. As for his popularity, he is without question one of the most liked people on staff. The same is true for his entire family. But looking back on the process now, I'm glad that I took the time to reflect on a potential area where fear could have undermined what has become a great fit.

Getting a Handle on It

Fear can be a catalyst for positive action too. How many of us have been motivated to act because we fear a particular outcome. For instance, you might embark on an all night study binge because you've just found out that you could possibly fail if you don't do well on the exam; or on a grander scale, a country that puts its citizens on alert and fortifies its borders because of the hostile provocations of a neighboring nation. Part of the management needed for a characteristic like fear is to use it to fuel your strengths, convictions, and passions, and not allow it to undermine you by becoming a Trojan Horse.

Definitions of fear abound but one of the more basic ones is that fear is a danger signal.[4] It alerts us to impending harm, triggers an adrenaline increase and heightens our sense of awareness. Fear is typical of most human characteristics, in that there are both good and bad aspects. In those circumstances when fear works in a positive or protective way, it serves well the purpose for which it was originally intended.

But fear in many instances plays a far larger role in our psyche. Though fear can serve a noble purpose, for many it becomes the most debilitating part of their ability to move forward in significant ways. Unless we learn ways to recognize and then face our fears, rarely are we able to get beyond its shackles. In fact, stagnant lives are primarily the result of becoming comfortable with being comfortable. Unless we allow ourselves to risk, and to leap into the unknown from time to time, we will never be able to face the prospect of our fears, let alone be able to have the courage to lead others through significant change.

Most effective leaders can easily be identified by one characteristic, that being courage. They are the ones who are first to step up and tackle a problem. It may be they are the only ones who seem to have any confidence in what to do next, and not only that, but are willing to make it happen.

It's not that most leaders who have left a mark on this world don't struggle with fear, it's that they have learned to face it courageously. Put another way, the leaders with the greatest impact are those that have learned to use fear to their advantage. They become more fearful of missed opportunities than they are the fear of failure. And when fear is understood in this way, to not act is to fail every time, without even trying.

It is for this reason that many of the more successful organizations and teams have a healthy understanding of failure and why they need to foster an environment that allows for people to take risks. Otherwise, fear of failure becomes the silent mantra, the deadly yet unspoken rule that governs the way decisions are made.

From my experience in observing leaders it is the ones who are action-oriented that are set apart. And I don't mean action just for action sake, but deliberate, purposeful action that initiate and motivate positive change and growth. It is these leaders who are able to identity and clarify problems, and find ways to move past them. They recognize that in order to keep fear from gaining a foothold, they need to confront it. The discipline of a leader becomes critical, because the more chaotic a situation becomes, the greater propensity for fear, and without the discipline to weather the storm; we end up becoming a victim of the circumstances.

Now this doesn't mean that the astute leader doesn't recognize the power of consensus, strategy, gaining trust, or diligent investigation. But the leader who is truly aware knows how to distinguish between fear and constructive data. One is helpful and one is hurtful, and if you want to grow, it means some sort of change is being proposed which invariably will expose whatever fears are prevalent. Most successful leaders don't lack fear. They just manage to find a way to act and persevere in spite of it.

Out of the Shadows

Another role that fear plays is its tendency to cause us to over-compensate. It may not be something you are easily aware of, but often those closest to you can see it. Let's say you have a fear of being overlooked or not recognized for the contributions you make. You will likely over-compensate with self-promotion. To the casual observer they will see you as possibly shallow and self-serving, regardless of your talents and abilities.

Maybe your fear is being poor and destitute. Your desire to counter that fear would likely be expressed in a hesitancy to give, or to be less than generous in your giving, which would appear to most as greed. This is one of our cultural phobias if there ever was one. We have created such a climate of fear surrounding the issue of money in North America that it manifests itself in greed. And greed is one of the most difficult vices to identify because it can mask itself so easily behind facades of being prudent, responsible, and faithful, when in reality it's greed generated by fear.

An interesting parallel happens in the church world around spiritual gifts, those supernatural abilities that every believer receives as part of their contribution to the whole. What I've noticed is that one way to identify a person's spiritual gift is to observe what it is that frustrates them. For instance, if someone has the gift of giving, often they will feel a continual frustration of not being able to exercise that gift more. Their resources limit their generosity even though they have a tremendous capacity to give.

The danger lies when they attempt to compromise their integrity to garner resources in order to feed their gift. That is nothing more than a shortcut to trouble. I once knew someone who gave away almost ninety percent of their income. It was amazing to watch. They did not lack for anything, yet had this staggering capacity to give most of what they made away.

But over time I came to see the down side. Though incredibly generous, they struggled whenever difficulty came into their life. They felt that because of their generosity they should be absolved of anything that would be hurtful or painful. Their anger at God in those moments was difficult to witness. In fact, they believed that their generosity excused them from other issues that God would not have approved of. They had significant sins that they were blind to. The person's total faith and service to God revolved around one inherent strength and gift, but with it came a very dark side as well.

So then, what do we do with fear? How do we bring it out of the shadows and expose it for what it is? And how do we protect ourselves from it becoming a Trojan Horse? How do we allow its awareness to fortify our strengths and not debilitate them? There are countless resources to help you navigate the minefield of fear.

I don't want to be cavalier about this problem because for many, it's very real. Nor do I want to say that you can manage it overnight with a few quick tips. I knew a counselor who adamantly asserted that he could cure any fear in thirty days. That may be true but for our purposes here I wanted to give you three steps as a starting point here and now.

The first is to *Identify*. Be open about what it is you fear. You may know this instinctively yet have never identified it in concrete terms. Don't just generalize them, be specific. Recognize those situations and circumstances that generate fear for you. Becoming fully aware of those moments that trigger your fear can help you from allowing that fear to dictate your responses.

The second is to **Clarify**. Why do you have those fears? Why is it that certain situations cause anxiety for you? Does the fear have a history? Knowing the why can invariably help you identify certain scenarios that you know will be problematic even before they occur.

The third is to **Quantify**. After identifying your fears and clarifying them, the next step is to ask, "What can I do about it?" Now the range of options here is virtually endless because it could mean anything from professional counseling to total avoidance. For many of our fears there are a host of mechanisms for coping and managing them, while at the same time not allowing them to rule you. It's here that the successful leader is able to leverage their fear in a positive way.

How does this work in the real world? Let me give you an example. Suppose your church is convinced that God is directing you to start an alternate service. Your leadership is keen on it but it's something your church has never tried before. You've done your research and from all accounts it's a good idea. In fact, as far as you're concerned it would be disobedient to God not to launch this project.

No matter how great the moral conviction to launch something new, the reality is these are the kinds of initiatives that can become derailed because of fear. It doesn't take long before the fears begin to be expressed. And here is an important point to note, it is not a bad thing that these fears are coming to the surface now. They are part of the process. An astute leader is one who recognizes them for what they are.

This is going to be a big change for the church. It will affect everything, so fear is a natural response. Not only that, it's also legitimate. There is a lot riding on this so how can it best be navigated. The problem is not to become so transfixed on the fear that it becomes the determining factor to the decision. First, let's identify the fears and list them:

- Fear of failing. This is new and unknown territory so the fear of it not succeeding is valid.
- Fear of changing the way things are. Many will be comfortable with the present situation, and may not even see the benefits of changing, so anything that upsets what's comfortable will be unwelcome.
- Fear of what it will cost. Not only in terms of finances, but also in staffing, building maintenance and cost, wear and tear, volunteers and so forth. To some it will be hard to rationalize the expenditure financially and the cost in time and human resources.

There may be others based on the particular specifics of your church or organization but those are likely the big ones. The next thing is to clarify the "why" behind those fears. Many of these will be personal and motivated primarily by the individual's fears for the most part. The list above best represents the collective fears of the church as a whole, while taking the time to clarify the fear deals with the personal anxieties of the project. The list could look something like this:

- People will fear that more will be asked of them, both from a financial and volunteer standpoint.
- Some will be uncomfortable with the risk. Why jeopardize the present reality with something that is untried and untested?
- There will be those who do not want to reach others and do not want to grow. Frankly, it was really painful for me to write that sentence, but sadly, they do exist.

These are the fears that will undermine the ability to raise funds or enlist volunteers. A leader's ability to assuage those fears and allay them by stressing the importance of the new opportunity cannot be understated. The moral compulsion and godly prompting must be greater than the collective fear of not doing it. One of the more prudent ways for a leader to proceed is through the third quantification step which helps to deal with the fears that have been expressed. Here are some examples of what it may look like:

- Announce it as a six month trial, after which the entire service will be evaluated. Make sure to add criteria for evaluation that is real and measurable but not so concrete that you become handcuffed to unreasonable projections. At the very least you want to be able to rationalize and justify your next steps.
- Cost it out for all to see. What will be the cost for the first six months? If the service ends up being cancelled, how long would it take the church to recoup that money?
- Ask the "worse case scenario" question. One of the best ways of alleviating people's fears at the beginning of a project is to ask this question. If everyone is aware of what the worst case scenario is should you have to shut it down after six months, the criticism and potential fallout is minimal primarily due to the fact that it did not come as a surprise to anyone.

A leader's two greatest enemies are perception and expectations. Both are ripe for fostering fear. The exercise above helps to manage both with intent and purpose. There is nothing like a successful project to alleviate people's fears. But between the genesis of an idea to the day it is considered a success, fear has plenty of room and time to play.

Every decision is fraught with potential failure, yet a smart leader doesn't ignore the fear but meets it head on. The strength of a church is in the people working together to accomplish God's Kingdom purposes. And yet many times, the church has allowed fear to dominate its mandate. Fear of culture, fear of change, fear of each other, and the list goes on.

Putting Fear Where it Belongs

Jesus, when traveling through Caesarea Philippi with his disciples asked them what the gossip mill was saying about him. Who did they think Jesus was? A prophet from the past or maybe even John the Baptist. When Jesus turns the question onto his disciples, Peter's answer seals his place in biblical history with the proclamation that Jesus is the long awaited Messiah, the Son of the living God.

Beyond the affirmation of Peter's revelation, Jesus unveils at that moment a declaration that still stands today. Here is what Jesus promised:

> Now I say to you that you are Peter, and upon this rock I will build my church, and all the powers of hell will not conquer it. (Matthew 16:18)

Think about what Jesus says here. The most antagonistic force against God in the universe, Hell itself, would not be able to thwart the church. Most people don't give Hell a second thought, but Jesus, aware of the battle between good and evil, makes a fearless proclamation about the future of the church. When God's people, armed with God's Spirit, moving in God's power, acting for God's purposes, are able to relegate fear to a position of not having any power over us it is unimaginable what can be accomplished.

Whenever leaders make decisions that are based in fear, it usually does two things. It gives you more of what you presently have, and secondly only raises the level of anxiety more. As Seth Godin writes, "Anxiety is practicing failure in advance."[5] Anxiety and fear, for all of their protective qualities in terms of guarding us from ever-present danger, can also keep us from exploring life beyond the confines of our cocoons.

Whether it's an individual, church, organization, or international conglomerate, fear has a way of undermining progress, growth, and positive change. It doesn't matter if we are talking about spiritual matters or board room politics, fear, left unchecked, will diminish the effectiveness of any organization. It would be interesting if we could ever survey the history of "what if's". Even if it were in one category alone, say the business world, the weight of responses to the simple prompting of "what if" would likely overwhelm us by the sheer volume.

When our sons, Michael and Jason were younger, my wife Darlene and I had a simple rule. They were never allowed to use the word, can't. Whenever we caught them using the word, we made them rearrange the sentence in order to avoid using it. It became a way of reinforcing in them the idea that, can't, simply lends itself to fear and defeat. Not only that, but it forced them to see the situation that prompted them to use the word as an opportunity, and it helped them to begin to formulate potential options for resolving it, as opposed to giving in before even trying. It served as one of the most important character development tools we could have instituted and something we didn't fully grasp at the time.

Lastly, applying "can't" to a situation discounts God. Especially since God specializes in the impossible, those very situations that prompt many of us to use "can't" in the first place. Darlene and I never wanted our sons to ever miss an opportunity due to fear or anxiety. It wasn't that we wanted them to ignore those feelings or those promptings, but to invariably trust God more.

Fear is one of the most potent Trojan Horses, and anytime you allow fear to diminish your capacity to lead from your strengths, it undermines your ability to lead well, or to lead at all.

CHAPTER 4

The Rage of a Sage

Since then, no prophet has risen in Israel like Moses, whom the Lord knew face to face... (Deuteronomy 34:10a)

Few figures in history loom as large as Moses, the man who confronted an Egyptian Pharaoh and led an entire nation out of slavery. Moses, the one who heard the call of God from a burning bush and became a nation's liberator and spiritual leader. A man who received from the hand of God the Ten Commandments that for centuries have served as the foundational precepts of the Western World.

Even Jesus, thousands of years later, would be compared to the legendary stature of Moses as he confronted the religious leaders of his day. Jesus, the incarnate Son of God, the second person of the Trinity, had to deal with comparisons to Moses, even though it only demonstrated just how misguided the religious leaders of the time were.

Nevertheless, the spiritual legacy that is Moses is without question. Even from his birth, he seemed marked for greatness. The Book of Exodus recounts a Pharaoh's anxiety at the rapid growth of the Hebrew slaves, causing him to demand the killing of any newborn male child. Upon his birth, Moses' parents recognized that he was no ordinary child and hid him for three months. When hiding was no longer an option they placed him in a basket and sent it down the

Nile, and in a moment of incredible providence, the child was found by the very daughter of Pharaoh.

What happens next is almost beyond belief. She enlists a Hebrew slave to raise the child, who happens to be Moses' real mother and even pays her for raising him! How sweet is that? When Moses is old enough, she returns him to Pharaoh's daughter to be raised in the shadow of the king's own household.

Without a doubt, the first 40 years of Moses' life is a contrast of experiencing firsthand the tension of masters over slaves. Very few in all of history would have understood more clearly or more profoundly the injustice of the master-slave relationship. On one hand, Moses would have benefitted from his place as an adopted member of Pharaoh's household, yet all the while feeling remorse over the state of those with who he shared a common heritage.

It's this gnawing tension that must have come to a head when Moses one day observes an Egyptian beating one of the Hebrew slaves. Exodus 2:11 tells us that Moses would go out and observe the Hebrews as they suffered under their hard labour. We can only imagine what must have been happening inside as he watched the abuse of his own people. Who knows how many times he would have murmured to himself that he wished he could do something to alleviate their plight. How long had the desire been simmering to change their circumstances until it became an imperative in his life?

Whatever it was that was roiling inside it finally compelled Moses to act. A decision that would alter his life forever. With no one looking, Moses murdered the offending Egyptian and buried him in the sand. However, whatever satisfaction he received from that act was short-lived. The very next day he saw two of the Hebrew slaves fighting and tried to intervene, but both men turned on Moses.

In a moment of horror he comes to realize that his actions in the murder of an Egyptian did not go unnoticed. Not only that, any hope of the act garnering him favors with the slaves is quickly dashed. From there the situation worsens. The deed has reached the ear of Pharaoh who has now put a price on Moses' life, one which forces him to escape into the desert and begin a forty year exile in the land of Midian.

What's Behind the Smoke?

Imagine for a moment living under the roof of a Pharaoh? It would be a life of luxury and opulence. Every possible social, economic, or educational advantage would be available and Moses would have easily been a benefactor of these privileges. But what was it inside of him that would cause him to put all of that in jeopardy for the sake of those slaves?

Though these were people related to him by blood and nationality, something more has to motivate someone to move with such compulsion. There are many throughout history who likely found themselves in the same circumstances as Moses, but history has forgotten them because of their inaction. What is it about a man like Moses who, regardless of the privileges he enjoys, risks it all for a greater moral imperative?

What is also of interest is the fact that the early years as recorded in the Bible show no hint of Moses having any relationship with the God of the Hebrews. His family would have likely been in continual prayerfulness for him, but Moses himself would have also been inundated with the Egyptian pantheon of gods. This would have been a point of contrast, the worship of the Hebrew slaves of the one God of Abraham, Isaac, and Jacob, over the hundreds that made up the Egyptian roster of deities.

The contrasts are so great in the life of Moses that they are too hard to ignore. Raised by his mother who was a slave, he would have witnessed firsthand the tyranny of that slavery. Further, the faith of her people would also likely have been a significant part of his upbringing. In Moses' mind the faith of the Hebrews in an all powerful God, whose lives were characterized by slavery may have seemed of little import in contrast to the might of Egypt and the regiment of gods they had at their disposal.

It seems these lessons were not lost on Moses as he transitioned from a home of slavery into a home of privilege. He never forgot where he came from and likely did not forgot the God that his ancestors imparted to him in his youth. It may have taken him forty years to act, but when he did, it was an expression of his anger at the injustice of the world he was a part of. Something that had been kindling inside of him for a long time.

Contained Dynamite!

The story of Moses taking the life of an Egyptian in Exodus 2 introduces us to a key personality trait inherent in Moses-his anger. As we will see, this part of his personality appears in a number of strategic moments in his story. Whenever it is fuelled by good intentions and honorable purposes it serves to motivate, inspire, and confront. But in those moments when his anger gets the better of him, the destruction it causes is great. Even to Moses himself.

The Hebrew word for anger is based on the idea of a fire burning or an inferno. It can denote the picture of a searing in the throat or the heat felt by a rage that makes the nostrils flare and the face turn red. In fact, the common Hebrew word for anger is also used for nose and face, often coupled with the word for kindle. In many instances it implies that the heat has been simmering for a period of time until that moment when the lid comes totally off. The imagery of a volcano is an appropriate one.

Many times in the stories of Moses the text reveals his mood as angry. It is a distinct marker in his makeup. For good or ill, anger is a common byproduct in the life of this man. The killing of the Egyptian by Moses in Exodus 2 is the beginning of a life marked by anger. In Exodus 11, when Moses is delivering the final warning to Pharaoh, the tenth plague that kills all the firstborn in Egypt, verse 8 concludes with the phrase, "Then burning with anger, Moses left Pharaoh."

The time between Exodus 2 and Exodus 11 is a little over 40 years, most of it spent in the land of Midian where Moses tended sheep, got married, settled done and raised a family. Yet, as the years progressed, nothing seems to have tempered his potential for anger. What marks those 40 years, though, is an encounter he has with God in the burning bush, one that sets the entire course of Moses' later life.

Despite the incredible call of God on his life, anger continues to be a problem for Moses. One example is found in Exodus 17 the people are pressing him for water because they are parched. Another is Numbers 11 where Moses is angry with God for being given the burden of responsibility over the Israelites. Their whining has exasperated not only the patience of Moses, but of God as well. In his rant towards the Lord, Moses wishes that God would strike him down and relieve him of his misery.

Moses heard all the families standing in the doorways of their tents whining, and the Lord became extremely angry. Moses was also very aggravated. And Moses said to the Lord, "Why are you treating me, your servant, so harshly? Have mercy on me! What did I do to deserve the burden of all these people? Did I give birth to them? Did I bring them into the world? Why did you tell me to carry them in my arms like a mother carries a nursing baby? How can I carry them to the land you swore to give their ancestors? Where am I supposed to get meat for all these people? They keep whining to me, saying, 'Give us meat to eat!' I can't carry all these people by myself! The load is far too heavy! If this is how you intend to treat me, just go ahead and kill me. Do me a favor and spare me this misery!" (Numbers 10:11-15)

At a time where most of us in this situation of feeling beaten and discouraged would turn to God for help, Moses lashes out in anger. Yes, you're right, he is essentially asking for help, but the 'request' is made in an angry and frustrated way. The burden that Moses feels has overwhelmed him to the degree of lashing out at God. It is almost surprising to recall that this is the same Moses who years earlier longed for these same Hebrews to be free.

In the Heat of the Moment

There are two significant stories that need mentioning regarding Moses and anger. The first is found in Exodus 32. This is a legendary passage and one of the defining moments in the life of Moses. The scene is Mount Sinai, the mountain of God. In Exodus 24 Moses has climbed to where a cloud has engulfed the summit. For six days Moses patiently waited, but on the seventh the Lord called him into the cloud. From the ground, the Israelites observing the cloud saw it as a fire that was consuming the summit. For forty days and forty nights the people waited and wondered, "What happened to Moses?"

For the next seven chapters, God and Moses have one of the most important religious meetings that history has ever known. It is here that God instructs him on the architecture of the Tabernacle and everything related to it. In addition to instructions concerning priests and their responsibilities came specifications for their garments, the naming of craftsmen, and a reminder on the importance of the Sabbath. Much transpired between God and Moses in those forty days and nights. But most of all, this is where God takes two tablets of stone, and with his very own finger, engraves upon them the Ten Commandments.

Now this is an incredibly profound meeting, and one that you wouldn't think God would take kindly to having interrupted. But that is exactly what happens. In chapter 32 we get a view of what is transpiring on the ground. The people, in their impatience, demand that Moses' brother Aaron build them "some gods" that can lead them. They obviously feel that Moses is likely never coming back. Aaron relents and ends up melting the gold jewelry of the people, constructing a golden calf complete with its own altar.

Meanwhile, God is fully aware of what is going on and tells Moses to take care of it before God annihilates them. Imagine the scene for a moment. God interrupts their meeting to make Moses aware of what is happening. In a beautiful example of the all-knowing nature of God, He even gives Moses the specifics of the crisis in the Israelite camp.

In the midst of this God even interjects that he has no problem starting over with Moses if necessary. Undoubtedly this was a test. One that Moses passes to the great relief of the people below who are unaware of his actions on their behalf. Yet here is the place that becomes common ground for this great man of God, serving as a mediator between an angry Lord and a sinful people.

Here is where the story gets interesting. Moses, with tablets in tow, begins down the mountain. Now, remember, he has spent forty days and nights in the presence of God, the creator of everything. Few, since the time of Adam and Eve have spent this kind of quality time with the Creator of the universe! Not only that, he holds in his possession, the only words etched by the very finger of God. Here are the only Scripture ever given that was not mediated through a human agent. These are directly from God. In light of this, look at what happens in verse 19 of Exodus 32:

When they came near the camp, Moses saw the calf and the dancing, and he burned with anger. He threw the stone tablets to the ground, smashing them at the foot of the mountain. (Exodus 32:19)

As Moses comes upon the scene he is aghast at the sight of the revelling. He burns with anger and does the unthinkable. He smashes the tablets and enters into a rampage. So much so that he takes the golden calf, burns it, grinds it into powder, throws it in the water and makes everyone drink it. If that isn't enough, he orders the unfaithful culprits to death and some 3000 are killed.

What is intriguing to me is Moses' response. I understand what the people did was unthinkable, but what was with the smashing of the tablets? Really? Did God not tell Moses what was happening before he went to see for himself? Did God not even go as far as tell Moses that it was a golden calf that had become their deity of choice?

And yet, even with that information in hand, and even after spending all that time in the presence of God, Moses takes whatever he can get his hands on to demonstrate his rage. And so, regardless of the worth of these tablets, they become insignificant in the face of the anger that spews out of Moses. Could he not have taken a moment to set them down first, especially since God himself told him what to expect? Did Moses think that God was lying or even exaggerating?

Imagine the care the art community would take if the Mona Lisa had to be moved to another location. Consider the security and the detailed planning that would go into making its transfer as smooth and as safe as possible. Yet here is Moses, with the very words of God in his hands and they become the casualties of a temper tantrum. I personally cannot imagine a clearer demonstration of Moses' problem with anger than what is shown here.

In the aftermath of this the judgement of God weighs heavy on the people. Moses, when his anger subsides, intercedes for the people.

When some semblance of order returns we come upon chapter 34. Look at the first four verses.

> Then the Lord told Moses, "Chisel out two stone tablets like the first ones. I will write on them the same words that were on the tablets you smashed. Be ready in the morning to climb up Mount Sinai and present yourself to me on the top of the mountain. No one else may come with you. In fact, no one is to appear anywhere on the mountain. Do not even let the flocks or herds graze near the mountain." So Moses chiseled out two tablets of stone like the first ones. Early in the morning he climbed Mount Sinai as the Lord had commanded him, and he carried the two stone tablets in his hands. (Exodus 34:1-4)

This story demonstrates a wondrous truth about God. He is well aware of Moses' problem with anger. And here, rather than God supplying the stone tablets like the first time he commands Moses to chisel them out for himself. I contend this is God's way of teaching Moses a lesson. One which would reinforce the detrimental effects of his anger and the consequences it brings. Every hammer blow of that chisel would be a means of remembering what Moses had done with the originals.

Anger Mis-management

One of the most beautiful passages in the Old Testament follows on the heels of this lesson. Moses, though he has spent countless moments in the presence of God, yearns for more. He asks if he can see God's glory. An opportunity to see the full manifestation of God beyond the snippets he has received thus far. And God complies to a degree by allowing Moses to see him as he passes by. As Moses awaits the sight, God covers the face of the prophet and releases it as He passes by. Moses gets to see the backside of God.

As God passes, he calls out what constitutes a short resume. The opening section is of particular importance here:

Yahweh! The Lord! The God of compassion and mercy! I am slow to anger and filled with unfailing love and faithfulness. (Exodus 34:6b)

Did you read that? God is slow to anger. Though God is seen from time to time as being angry with the people, His anger is distinctly different from Moses. God's anger is measured, tempered, specific, and justified. Sin is no laughing matter, especially to God. Even though there are moments when God must act, they are preceded by long pauses not instant retribution. And lastly, God is God. Only God has the moral capacity to manage anger perfectly, something that we cannot humanly hope to fully understand. I wonder if part of the reason God chooses to state this is to reinforce his earlier lesson to Moses, and to give him pause for the way he manages anger.

Certainly Moses, though a man used mightily of God, struggles with anger containment. Don't misunderstand, there are times in his life where the heat that anger generates becomes a catalyst for good. Unfortunately, that same energy in other situations becomes too volatile and harmful, so much so in fact that it eventually becomes his undoing.

In Numbers 20 we have an all too common scene. The people are once again griping. This time it's a shortage of water. In typical response, Moses, along with his brother Aaron, asks God for a miracle. They are given specific instructions to take the staff of Moses and to speak to a nearby rock which will yield the much needed water. But when Moses calls the people he rebukes them and then proceeds to strike the rock twice. Rather than speaking to the rock as God directed, Moses instead rants at the people and takes out his frustration on the rock-countering the instructions God had given him.

At first glance this seems harmless enough. The water flows and the need is satisfied. But for Moses and Aaron, the irreverence shown for God is too great. Moses' anger has once again gotten him into trouble, but this time it will cost him. God promptly announces that neither men will enter the Promised Land. Aaron as the High Priest, and Moses as the Prophet and leader of God's people, demonstrated the most grievous act of disobedience. One witnessed in the presence of the entire congregation of Israel.

The life of Moses is bracketed by two poor anger management moments. The first in the murder of an Egyptian that propels him into a forty year exile, to the last one which put him in direct defiance of God. What results is almost hard to imagine. The very purpose for which Moses has been enlisted, will come to fruition without him. As the nation of Israel enters the land of Promise it will do so without the man who has led it since the Exodus.

God does allow Moses a final look. In the land of Moab he climbs Mount Nebo on the eastern border of the Promised Land and Moses scans the vista before him. The scene is recounted in Deuteronomy 34. From his mountaintop vantage point Moses can see the land that his people will soon occupy. What began many years earlier in the land of Egypt has now come to this moment. Moses, who longed for the liberation of his people, can now die confident in its realization.

The Book of Deuteronomy concludes with a summary of the life of Moses:

> There has never been another prophet like Moses, whom the LORD knew face to face. The LORD sent Moses to perform all the miraculous signs and wonders in the land of Egypt against Pharaoh, all his servants, and his entire land. And it was through Moses that the LORD demonstrated his mighty power and terrifying acts in the sight of all Israel. (Deuteronomy 34:10-12)

Moses' epitaph clearly places him in a league that few can rival. Nonetheless, due to his anger, the epitaph comes sooner than Moses likely hoped. Imagine that for forty years, Moses trudged through the desert with the hopeful expectation of one day seeing the land flowing with milk and honey. Yet here he is viewing it some moments before his death from the summit of a neighbouring mountain.

The very character quality that ignited a fire within Moses to confront injustice, lead a nation, stand strong during adversity, and motivate a people to holy living, becomes the very quality, when unbridled, that brings this giant of faith down.

The book of Deuteronomy contains Moses' final instructions to the people before entering the Promised Land. Throughout its pages one can feel the prophet's residual anger. These people, who he has led for all these years have been his undoing. They brought him to fits of frustration and anger, so much so, that at a weak juncture in his life, he responded in a fit of rage that not only caused him grief with the people, but with God as well.

Who's to Blame?

Like every emotion, anger is God given. As with any emotion, what was originally meant for good, became distorted by the Fall. Though anger itself is not sinful, how we use it and express it is where the trouble happens. It often points to deeper problems-an emotional wound, a personal violation, an unrealized hope. As natural as this emotion may be, it has great potential to cause harm.

For most of his life, Moses was a righteous man, and it could be argued that his anger was an expression of his righteous indignation. That may be true for the most part, but what roiled inside of him as righteous conviction, eventually became the vehicle that led him into direct disobedience of God.

We can never deny Moses' love for and commitment to God, nor that God accomplished mighty things through him. But the story of Moses reminds us once again of our human frailties and their capacity to undermine even our best intentions. His life is one of history's most instructive in terms of leadership. Responsible for overseeing a nation, whose sole reason for existence was to demonstrate the supremacy and holiness of the one true God, the life of Moses was anything but easy.

The greatest source of anxiety for Moses wasn't necessarily his responsibility before God, as daunting as that was, but the ongoing conflict and disobedience of the people. They became his greatest source of frustration. Time and again they would fail in their loyalty to God which would result in their chastening. Their ongoing complaints must have taken a toll on Moses as each season brought new and more inventive ways for the people to whine and defy God.

The very people who Moses was called to lead, were the very people who exasperated him to such a degree that he lost it. At a critical juncture his frustration with them resulted in his losing sight of God's requirements and focusing his anger on the people. It is hard to fathom that some eighty years earlier, Moses struck down an Egyptian because he grieved at the plight of the Hebrews. Now having seen their liberation realized, these same Hebrews become a critical factor in his downfall.

Here is where the life of Moses serves as an example to anyone in leadership. The very people to whom we have a responsibility, are often our greatest source of frustration. Anyone who has spent time in the leadership trenches can attest to this fact. Whether it's a congregation or the marketplace, the very people we either serve or sell to, can exasperate us the most. If were not careful, our sense of frustration can eventually fuel an anger that could erupt at a most inopportune moment. And just like Moses, we can soon find ourselves in trouble.

CHAPTER 5

The Trojan Horse of Anger

"Anybody can become angry — that is easy, but to be angry with the right person and to the right degree and at the right time and for the right purpose, and in the right way — that is not within everybody's power and is not easy." Aristotle

My wife and I took a trip to visit our oldest son Michael who lives in London, England. We love the city and the richness of its history and culture. On one particular day we were enjoying our usual walk about in an area of the city that had me doing my best to capture the vista before us. It was classic Britain, with its busses, cabbies, telephone booths, you name it. I'm sure that every person within a hundred yards knew that we were tourists, at least with respect to me.

As we were enjoying the ambience of a warm, sunny afternoon, the bustle of the street was broken by the shrill sound of a woman's voice. It was jarring. We all stopped to look around and see what prompted the outburst. I was expecting to have seen the aftermath of an accident, or a mugging, or something along those lines because the harshness of the screaming was now echoing between the buildings on either side of the street.

As our eyes fixed on the source, to our amazement was this young girl who was in full decibel throttle screaming at some young man. My assumption was almost immediate: Boyfriend. Had to be. Rightly or wrongly, that was the safest bet, and I sure wasn't going near them to have that question clarified. So, with that assumption firmly in my head, I wondered what could have happened to prompt such a public display of anger.

I personally get very curious at those moments. What did he say, or what did he do? Boy, was she steamed! Last we saw they were getting on a bus together while she was in mid insult. I can't imagine what the driver and those passengers had to put up with. Whatever it was that sparked such venom must have been very serious. After-all, an entire block of a busy British street became an unwilling audience to the drama unfolding between this young couple.

Now I have no idea what caused the outburst, and the young man could very well have deserved and even invited the anger, but whatever it was, it caused a young woman to vent without any regard for the arena in which the drama unfolded.

Keeping a Lid on It

We have all been in situations when anger got the best of someone. We've watched as people have come unraveled before our very eyes. I remember walking into a home and seeing a distinct hole in the wall. The response from the person was simply, "Don't ask," and the rest was understood.

You are probably reading this right now and recounting a time or two when anger got the best of you. Surprising how it does that. You've even experienced someone else having a meltdown and the subsequent embarrassment you felt for them. We've all been in both scenarios. Whenever anger grips us, our actions seem warranted in the moment, but when we experience it in others, it can be humiliating.

Anger has a way of making us forget, temporarily, the priorities of objectivity. In an instant, it can deconstruct what we've worked so hard to build. Even in those moments when we can justify and ratio-nalize our anger the damage it can cause is quick and thorough.

I've been asked a number of times about the stress I experience in my vocation as a pastor. The assumption behind the question is always the same. "How can you handle being with people and their problems to the degree you are and keep it together?" Instinctively, we all know that people will be people, and the more people involved, the more potential for problems.

No doubt they are focusing on the negative side of the equation. As true as it is at times, there are many moments when it's a joy to serve people. But we all know that it's the difficult people who tend to raise our blood pressure and escalate the potential for frustration. In fact, if truth be told, those moments serve as nothing more than con-tinual reminders that we live in a fallen world and it's consequences are all around us.

For those who have asked, once they hear what my greatest source of stress is, they always knowingly nod in agreement. It's not the nature of pastoral ministry per se, nor the weight of responsibil-ity that elevates my anxiety. It's situations where ongoing negativity, nagging, and whining are allowed to become the loudest voices in our heads.

It's in those moments of frustration that Moses' story resonates most with me. It is one thing to bear the burden of responsibility, it's quite another to be constantly under the weight of incessant com-plainers. Nothing seemed to make the people of Israel happy, and for a man like Moses who already struggled with anger issues, the con-stant needling was bound to take its toll.

I used to think that the primary reason for people's complaining was due to the lack of clear vision, which ultimately creates a vacuum of urgency that allows people to turn their attention inward rather than on the importance of a particular mission or objective. For some time I assumed this was a root cause. We hear all the time in the church world about the importance of vision and how that will quell most discontent. But the more I looked at the story of Moses the more it challenged that assumption.

Here was a nation that had been miraculously saved out of slavery. Envision what it would have felt like to finally be free of the shackles and the harshness of their bondage. They witnessed countless demonstrations of God's power, and all of it so he could plant them into a good and perfect land. I can't imagine a more inspiring vision to convey to a group of people than that. Yet despite this glorious future, they turned it into a fractured present, mostly due to their incessant complaining and lack of trust in God.

Every Fire Begins with a Spark

As far as I can tell, frustration doesn't get the respect it deserves. As we consider anger and its potential as a Trojan Horse, we can't ignore the role that frustration plays. One dictionary definition given was "the feeling of being upset or annoyed, primarily due to the inability to change or achieve something." I can't tell you how much that definition resonated with me when I read it, especially as a leader in a church where at times it can seem like endless dialogue is required just to get a single motion passed. Those moments are when you begin to get some idea of what Jesus meant by "weeping and gnashing of teeth."

Frustration, unguarded and unchecked, will at some point ignite a more intense amount of heat in you. Consider it an early warning system. From my experience, the longer a sense of frustration is allowed to ferment, the more likely that an eruption is just on the horizon.

That is not to say that everyone will follow this pattern. We are all wired uniquely and some are just able to handle their emotions and their anger in ways that others cannot. But if you have any similarity to Moses, then treat frustration with the respect it deserves.

I know that in the church world, frustration for leaders is a continual hazard. You simply cannot be with that many people for any length of time without someone poking you the wrong way. It's like the proverbial porcupine who longs to be intimate but the closer he gets to others the more his quills become a problem. I have served in churches where remarkable things were happening, exactly the kinds of wondrous phenomena that we long and pray for, while in the background there was this continual hum of dissension from some that never squared with the larger reality.

The danger here is to allow our frustration and anger to govern our emotions. We can even begin to "dehumanize" people because they do nothing more than frustrate us. It is incredibly difficult to look upon someone you have dehumanized with eyes of grace. Yes, I know, there really are evil people in the world, and some may be too close in proximity to you for your liking. But they are the exception, not the norm.

Anger can lend itself to becoming a form of internalized apathy and despair. If not careful, it can fester inside us when displeasure exists between God and the apparent way our lives are taking shape. I've seen this more times than I care to count. When life does not unfold in a good way, our tendency can be to blame God, which in time, left unchecked, will transform itself into loathing Him. And anger turned inward, characterized by despair and loathing, can often lead to depression.

An opposite danger exists as well. Those who live by strict adherence to God's ways can feel their values ridiculed and rejected by the culture at large. These are the tensions that can easily transform into righteous anger that escalates further into the persona of a warrior who is in a battle for God. We begin to view everything around us as

70

a direct attack on the values we hold dear, because we see them as an affront to God. This externalized anger often leads to some form of self righteous condemnation if not all out aggression.

Undoubtedly, the Bible advocates for anger that is directed at whatever makes God angry. Acts of injustice, greed, human exploitation, immorality, and so forth. They are justifiable objects for our wrath that should ignite in us a burden to face these head on and bring about positive change. But there's the rub, isn't it? Lurking in us, especially those who've become passionate about a cause, is the potential to turn the cause into a crusade. And if caution isn't exercised, the crusade can become consuming to the degree that you can lose focus, perspective, and even objectivity.

These are the inherent dangers of frustration and anger. The more they are allowed to ferment, the greater the propensity for an explosion. Here's why: frustration and anger in many ways signal in you the feeling that you are being robbed of something. It is the ultimate proclamation that says, "You Owe Me!"[1] It's a feeling that you deserve something you are not getting. And the longer those feelings continue, the greater your need to have them justified or satisfied.

It could be as simple and innocuous as missing your morning coffee, or as significant as the rejection of a major proposal at work-the reasons are as varied as the people on this planet. But for leaders in particular, the hazards of a growing entitlement fostered internally by anger is an especially dangerous place to be. When you begin to look at the very people you sell to or serve and see them as owing you something, it isn't difficult to make a prediction about how it's likely going to end.

Remember Moses? Things did not particularly end well for him. We are a bit uncomfortable to even mention that misstep. One that was so uncharacteristic for a man whose entire destiny was shaped by an unrelenting duty to follow God. But in a moment of anger, where all focus and reason were momentarily suspended, Moses acted grievously against God.

I don't want to proceed without stressing this next point. Despite Moses' tendency towards anger, he nevertheless stands in history as one of God's greatest servants. There is not the slightest doubt that God used Moses and acted through him to perform some of the most miraculous events ever. But don't believe for a second that the story of Moses, from his greatest achievements to his most devastating failures, isn't meant to teach us a lesson as well. If a man like Moses can fall, where does that leave me?

What the Bible continually reminds us of concerning the nature of humanity, is that we are forgetful and rebellious. And if you as a leader are in any way prone to frustration and anger, you need to find some way to constructively diffuse it.

Self …

Here is a little test I've used over the years. How would you fill in this blank? Self_____. From my experience let me propose a number of possibilities that likely came to mind. The more common ones are, self-serving, self-motivated, self-reliant, self-satisfied. These are the answers I typically receive. Primarily because they get the most air time in our social media saturated world.

In today's culture, our sense of self has become the centre of our proverbial universe. I've often joked with students that in the Middle Ages Copernicus and Galileo were attacked for positing the thesis that the earth revolved around the sun, a proposal that caused an uproar at a time when we believed the earth was the centre of the universe.

Fast forward to today and we've moved to the *self* as the centre of all things. Funny how that happens. But back to our question. How many would fill in the blank with the word "control." Now there's a concept; self-control. I can't say this is a trait that is actively advocated nowadays. I can't recall the last time I saw an advertisement promoting it. The current mantras of our society are, "You deserve the very best," or, "don't wait, do it now!" The very notion of self-control may be more foreign than an alien from the Alpha Centauri system.

We are taught to allow whatever impulses we have to dictate the way we live out our lives. But emotions by themselves are hardly the gauges we should be relying on. Rarely do our emotions evoke in us a sense of restraint and control. It's more like wild abandon. Many leaders intuitively make decisions from our gut. But what if the gut reaction is informed more by anger and frustration that has spawned in us a sense of entitlement?

Rage has become a normal fixture in our society. By all appearances we are growing in our sense of frustration and anger. More and more we hear of individuals taking matters into their own hands and expressing their anger through violent means. The very thought of someone walking into a school and opening fire upon other children was unfathomable when I was young. Yet in our present era, the incidence of such mindless destruction does not appear to be subsiding.

We've all heard of road rage, but now the description of rage is being attached to everything from air travel to seniors. Ever heard of Bridezilla? Having presided over two hundred weddings there is little I haven't experienced in that world. Frankly, as I look around, there is plenty to be angry about. It would be very easy to get up every morning and face the world in a rage because of all the problems that seem to surround us. If you are prone to anger and want to fuel your sense of frustration you won't have far to venture to get kindling.

Can government get your blood boiling? Let's dig deeper. What about taxes? If that doesn't start your heart into fits what about corporate greed. Been by a gas pump lately? Really? Gas has gone up again? Why? Because some narrow canal on the edge of the planet was flooded? Oh, by the way, that little strip of water really has nothing to do with the oil industry anyway. Talk about any excuse to financially pillage the average family just wanting to get by!

Okay, I think you get the point. Frustration, anger, rage, they all have their place, and there are lots of reasons to vent. But is that really where we want to park ourselves? So many live in a continual state of upheaval, and for a leader, any growing sense of despair at the conditions around him will lead to an unhealthy place in the end. In fact, history has proven time and again, that the ones who make the world a better place are the ones who refuse to let the circumstances around them determine the status-quo for their life.

Rarely a day goes by that I'm not confronted by someone who could potentially light a fire under me. I can't tell you the hurtful, painful, unjust, immoral, unhealthy, destructive, or simply unbelievable situations I come across that are coals just waiting for more fuel.

Here is what I believe is a key ingredient for the leaders who desire to be the best. They've learned to manage their frustrations and anger, or at the very least learned to channel them properly. It is easy, even to the point of being the default mode in some of us, to be angry at everything. If we look at the state of things around us and allow frustration at what we see to predominate our thoughts, we will eventually nurture a spirit of despair, apathy, and hopelessness. No one wants to follow a leader whose characterized in that way. I like the imagery in Proverbs 25:28:

A person without self-control is like a city with broken-down walls. (Proverbs 25:28)

The person who lacks self-control is likened to a city in ruins. Its broken walls leave the city exposed to the elements and to its enemies. Safety would be at a premium, which would lead to a state of fear and despair. In the ancient world the walls stood as the first line of defence, and without them, the entire population lay bare and exposed. Quite an image to convey of someone who is out of control.

Self-control in our culture is at a premium. And that is saying nothing about the way we treat morality, sexuality, or ethics. We are only applying it to the realm of anger. As mentioned earlier, we've all witnessed someone who lost it. Those moments are embarrassing. But for a leader, it can threaten the very effectiveness you may have otherwise. Nothing is more daunting than an employee who has to present bad news to an employer who is known for their fits and tirades. Remember the adage, "Don't shoot the messenger?"

Let me leave you with a couple of wise sayings from Proverbs before heading into the next section.

Fools vent their anger, but the wise quietly hold it back. (Proverbs 29:11)

An angry person starts fights; a hot-tempered person commits all kinds of sin. (Proverbs 29:22)

Protecting Your Voice

Now here is where I think a key point needs to be made. Every great leader must manage carefully the fuel that feeds anger and frustration. Any leader who is lifeless, without ambition, fire, conviction, vision, or energy, ever inspires anyone. They may get the minimum job done, but rarely do they leave a legacy of worth. Let alone serving as one to be emulated. They are likely better *de-motivators* than leaders who inspire followers into a brave new world.

Any leader worth following rarely stands for the status-quo. In fact, in all likelihood, it's their greatest source of angst. Change in any organization is difficult and the longer it has existed without a culture of change the more cemented and difficult it is to initiate.

That is where vision, mission, and core values become key for promoting change and direction. Leaders are not only seen as their representatives, but the primary torch-bearers. This is what I mean by a leader's voice.

In leadership it is important to maintain your voice. We all want to be heard, whether it is in a personal or business relationship, it is an important need in all of us. As a leader, your voice is one of your greatest tools. Now, you may say that no, it's not good enough to just say something, you need to be an example, someone who is a doer. And I would agree.

But what happens to a leader when suddenly no one is listening to you? Your effectiveness is gone, and any hope you had of bringing change has evaporated. The relationship you now have is characterized by mistrust and muddled sneers. Your voice, though not always the main reason you are a leader, is in most cases the first thing to be lost. It's true that many reasons exist for this scenario; anything from a leader's moral failure, poor judgement, bad decisions, toxic nature… any number of reasons can be posited for a leader losing his voice. But for my money, anger is one of the fastest ways to silence it.

As I write this there is a video that has gone viral of a pastor who has a meltdown in the midst of his message. I watched in horror as this man did and said the unthinkable. It has always been unwise to act out in this way, but in the social media age your mistakes become exposed to the entire world. I am still praying that the video was a hoax. Nevertheless it was a sober reminder of what can happen when frustration and anger get the best of us.

As a Pastor, the importance of protecting my voice is paramount. Each and every week I stand before a congregation and present a message primarily crafted through words. Words that bring the truth of Jesus and His work into the reality of people's lives. Words that bring healing, hope, and transformation. What would happen if suddenly no one was listening? Especially because of a momentary lapse of judgment on my part that was fuelled by anger or frustration.

I know this is a constant threat for every church communicator, and that the likelihood of people staying when you've lost your voice is remote, but that does not mean we do not maintain diligence regardless. I know that there have been times I've made unpopular decisions, and I have felt the unhappiness the following Sunday; but my prayer is that the moment I step up to give the message, those words are not lost because I have lost my voice.

This is frankly an issue that revolves mostly around the church world. I know that examples like Steve Jobs of Apple, don't square with what I've presented here. He was notorious for being brutally honest to the point of cruelty. He is just one of many example. But as leaders in the church, as examples of Christ to the world, are those the examples we want to emulate?

One of my greatest sources of grief is the degree in which the church has lost its voice to the culture in which we claim to minister. To be the repository of the greatest message the world has ever known and to barely make a dent into the moral and ethical climate of the times is a travesty to say the least. We are known more for what we are against as opposed to what we are about.

Could it be that we've allowed the wrong characteristics of what we represent to become the primary voice? Those of judgement, condemnation, accusation, and yes, maybe even anger? Now I'm not talking about shying away from speaking truth or challenging people in their sin or any of that. What I am saying is we often forget that how we say something is just as critical as what we say. And in many cases, the how has invalidated the what, because ears have already been shut.

Take a moment to reflect on this passage from Proverbs. I know that it has stopped me in my tracks many times.

A gentle answer deflects anger, but harsh words make tempers flare. (Proverbs 15:1)

Awareness

Awareness for a leader is critical. Frustration and anger can easily become one of the blind spots in a leader's life. You can allow yourself to become overwhelmed by the frustrations you experience, or you can intentionally do something to protect yourself. And the first thing I believe is identifying clearly the areas that cause you frustration.

Remember, frustration for many is an early warning signal, a kind of red alert that points to a potential blow up. Some frustrations are of course natural and easily managed, but it's the ongoing and significant ones that fuel the larger fireworks. You know what's really strange? The source of ongoing frustration and the eventual major blow don't even have to be related?

This happens in relationships all the time. You suddenly find yourself in a spat, only to find out later that something unrelated was the real thorn. This latest event only brought the matter to a head. When you sit down to talk it out you find out what the real reason for the conflict. Usually something unrelated to the latest dust up. We invariably end up asking questions like, "Why didn't you let me know?" or "You should have told me sooner." You get the picture.

When I began this project I felt compelled to write about the potential hazards that lurk behind our God-given strengths which we have been endowed that's due to our fallen nature. They can become the primary culprits when we fall. So let me at least leave you with a couple of helpful suggestions to get you started. Otherwise, if this is an area of concern for you, find help and do it now!

As I do so I want to direct you to a passage from the Book of Ephesians. The writer is the apostle Paul, and what he presents has great merit for our discussion.

> Get rid of all bitterness, rage, anger, harsh words, and slander, as well as all types of evil behavior. Instead, be kind to each other, tenderhearted, forgiving one another, just as God through Christ has forgiven you. (Ephesians 4:31-32)

Paul writes that we should get rid of, or remove from our lives, all bitterness, rage, anger, harsh words, and so on. Quite the passage from a guy who was writing this from a Roman prison. And what's with that little word, "all?" It doesn't leave much wiggle room does it? I like to call these "spotlight passages." They shine the spotlight on areas of life that for most of us are in need of work. But rarely do we like the spotlight on those areas because we're often uncomfortable with what is exposed.

But a leader's self-awareness in these areas is vital. A leader who struggles with frustration and anger will have to make as part of his regimen of self-awareness an acknowledgement of the potential triggers. Are there specific situations, people, places that provoke a spark? Are there physical or emotional cues that exist as your level of frustration escalates?

None of us would disagree that what Paul has listed here in the first sentence are all behaviours that cause relational tension and problems. That is why the spotlight can be so harsh. I would contend that on average, most of us can relate to the first set of behaviours more easily than the second set. At best we can say that we are moving in the direction of the second set.

Which leads us to those. Notice the second set begins with the word, "Instead." So, rather than act with anger, rage, etc., we should be forgiving, tenderhearted, and so forth. Actually, go back and read those two verses again and make sure you fully grasp the contrast.

I love what Paul does here, something that we all know instinctively in one form or another. In order to change a negative behaviour one of the best ways to do so is to replace it with a positive one. The second set of behaviours is a redirect. Take the energy spent on the negative behaviours and redirect it into these others. You're going to be expending emotional energy anyway, why not do so in a way that will be positive for your relationships.

We need to openly deal with our anger and not bury it. The stakes are too high. Beyond shining the spotlight on the problem and taking measures to channel your anger in productive ways, don't neglect to take the matter to God. Deep behavioural change does not happen without divine intervention. The best that we can humanly accomplish is re-formation, but only the Spirit of God can bring about transformation.

I want to once again challenge you with one of my favorite Proverbs, one that is bound to make you smile, as you begin to deal with your anger.

As the beating of cream yields butter and striking the nose causes bleeding, so stirring up anger causes quarrels. (Proverbs 30:33)

Anger can potentially become a Trojan Horse, and anytime you allow anger to diminish your capacity to lead from your strengths, it undermines your ability to lead well, or to lead at all.

CHAPTER 6

The Giant Within

But God removed Saul and replaced him with David, a man about whom God said, 'I have found David son of Jesse, a man after my own heart. He will do everything I want him to do.' (Acts 13:22)

His life takes up whole chapters from Samuel, Kings, and Chronicles, some sixty-two in all. The Bible's most read book, the Psalms, is primarily credited to him, which would make him one of history's most read authors. He is the Old Testament figure most mentioned in the New Testament with fifty-nine references and is one of the most endearing figures in Scripture as well as the forbearer of the Messiah, Jesus Christ.

David's life reads as a thesis for success. Israel's second King was known for his courage and strength in battle and as a wise leader of the nation. But his greatest accolade was this: He was a man after God's own heart. Now that is quite a claim to fame. To be known for your prowess in battle or for your musical talent is one thing, but to be characterized by your relationship with God is quite another.

Such a title would not have been given lightly. As King, there would have been many filters by which to measure him. His ability to govern, his expertise in battle, or even his tactical capability. And what of his reputation as Israel's brilliant songwriter, to say nothing of the judgment made upon him for the range of his moral and ethical integrity.

Yet despite all the potential labels that could have adorned this man, the one that has endured the most is his relationship with and heart for God.

Undoubtedly, the greatest impression left by David's life was not accomplishment or legacy oriented, but relationally oriented. His life was an expression of someone who had surrendered himself to the Lord. Despite his station in life and his many successes, their weight is measured through the lens of his love for God.

God greatly favored David and his life was richly blessed because of it. As we read through the biblical narrative of his life, it is continually framed in the context of David's faithfulness and love for God. And the relationship is not one-sided either. God not only recognized David's heart early on when he prompted Samuel to anoint him as Israel's king, but entered into a covenant with David. One that promised that his throne would not leave his family and from his lineage would come the long awaited Messiah, Jesus Christ.

The life of David is one of the most comprehensive stories told in Scriptures. Few get the kind of attention that David does, especially with such a wide lens. From his very public life, to the very intimate elements of his family life; from a young sheepherder to his final days on earth, nothing escapes the biblical biographer. His life serves as one of the best character studies, especially as we look at the very human trappings that comprise the man David, and the lessons we can glean from his life.

Early Warning Sign

The life of David begins almost like a fairy tale. Samuel, the Prophet, is commanded by God to go and anoint the next king of Israel. Saul, the nation's first monarch, has failed and been rejected, paving the way for a new king to be chosen. This time the selection process is one wholly initiated and confirmed by God, rather than at the behest of the people.

Samuel is directed to Bethlehem to seek out the house of Jesse, whose one son has been chosen by God as the next ruler. I find this part of David's story so intriguing. As Samuel is perusing the sons of Jesse in his home, he's thinking to himself that this crop of young men isn't bad! In fact, when he is presented with Eliab, the oldest, Samuel is convinced he is standing before Israel's next king. But his assumption is quickly dashed. In verse 7 of 1 Samuel 16 we read:

> But the LORD said to Samuel, "Don't judge by his appearance or height, for I have rejected him. The LORD doesn't see things the way you see them. People judge by outward appearance, but the LORD looks at the heart." (1 Samuel 16:7)

What is stressed as a criteria is not what we typically expect, nor what Samuel expected. But as all seven sons come forward, God rejects each one. Somewhat perplexed, Samuel asks the obvious question: "Are these all the sons you have?" What's revealed next is fascinating. David, the youngest of the brood hasn't even been presented. He is out tending the sheep.

Now I'm suspecting that Jesse had to make sure that his flocks were taken care of when the rest were attending to business, and who better than the youngest child? After all, in that culture the weight of responsibility and honor normally fell on the oldest son, so it was not unreasonable that Jesse would have expected his oldest, Eliab, to be first pick. Imagine the family's surprise when son after son gets passed over until finally, one last son remains.

Can I force a pause right now? Imagine for a moment what that household would be like? Seven sons have been rejected, and the man of God, Samuel, is in the living room having been commanded by God to anoint the next king from this family. How awkward would those moments be as the rest of the family waited as David was being fetched? What would they be thinking? What disbelief and shock would they be experiencing? How would they respond as they watched David get the nod? Here is where the story resumes:

> So Jesse sent for him. He was dark and handsome, with beautiful eyes. And the LORD said, "This is the one; anoint him." (1 Samuel 16:12)

Pretty much to the point. The passage continues from that brief note with Samuel anointing David among his brothers, where we are told that the Spirit of the Lord came powerfully upon David from that moment on. Although David was now anointed in the eyes of God, Samuel, and his family, the throne for which David was destined for would still be some time coming.

There is a little detail I want to go back to. Notice the description of David in the verse above. It describes him as dark, handsome, and having beautiful eyes. If there is one thing about the biblical writers I've learned it's that they do not squander or waste details. This is no different. Especially in a passage where God stressed the criteria as not being about external looks. Why give this description? Especially when it goes against the spirit of the passage.

Many gloss over this as nothing more than an elaboration but note, rarely does the Bible give details just for creative flare. You don't have biblical stories setting the mood with, "It was a dark and stormy night," unless they need to do so for a reason.

For instance, in Genesis 39:6 we are told that Joseph was a handsome and well-built young man. That detail sets up the story of Potiphar's wife lusting after Joseph. In Exodus 11:7, we are told that in the final plague upon Egypt, it would be so peaceful that not even a dog will bark. That little detail stresses the protective hand of God upon the Israelites on the very night the death angel visits Egypt. Imagine a night so calm that even the animals are untroubled.

So what do we make of this short description. Though it can appear as nothing more than a writer's embellishment, we will soon see that it foreshadows an area where David will struggle. A little precursor to a future problem for this newly anointed king.

The Making of a Hero

One of the more memorable stories of David in the Old Testament is his slaying of the giant, Goliath. Overnight, this virtual unknown is cast as a national hero, a victory that came at a time when David was barely old enough or tall enough to fit into normal battle attire. He therefore had to face Goliath without any protection or armour, with just a slingshot in his hand.

You can read the story for yourself and soak in all the details of the narrative, but for our purposes here I want to focus on a bit of an obscure passage. Again, we are not trying to discount the major narrative of David's life. He is one of the most celebrated figures of the Bible with much to commend. Yet even in this well known and iconic story of his defeat of a nine foot tall Philistine, David is beginning to battle a giant of another kind.

Just before David faces Goliath in the ultimate showdown, he is carousing with the men and his oldest brother sees him. This is what we read in verse 28 of 1 Samuel 17:

> But when David's oldest brother, Eliab, heard David talking to the men, he was angry. "What are you doing around here anyway?" he demanded. "What about those few sheep you're supposed to be taking care of? *I know about your pride and deceit.* You just want to see the battle!" (1 Samuel 17:28)

Now I've highlighted the portion I want to focus on. I've read many a commentator who correctly point out that this brother, Eliab, is the one who first got rejected to become king back in chapter 16. Therefore, it would stand to reason that poor Eliab has a bit of a chip when it comes to David. No doubt jealousy is playing a role here. Eliab must feel cheated by his youngest brother who has taken from him a prize that should have been his.

Many commentators give an idealized view of David here, and give little credence to Eliab's verbal jab. Eliab sees in David his sense of vanity and ambition. That's what he is prodding here. There is little doubt that in the heart of David is primary the glory of God and the honor of the Israelites; but in every act of glory lies a potential seed of hubris.

The Hebrew text is quite explicit. Eliab states, "I know!" He's not speaking from rumour or conjecture, but from personal observation and experience. This is no distant suspicion on his part. Further, "pride and deceit" denote in Hebrew the concepts of arrogance and wickedness or evil in heart. Even if these were exaggerations, they still reveal a potential that Eliab sees in David. Even at a time when David is about to accomplish an incredible triumph for God and country.

So for me, to argue that Eliab is venting his jealousy and leave it there is short-sighted. I don't know about your family dynamics, but whenever I got into a spat with my brother I didn't have to invent things. My brother could say the same about me. At any moment either one of us could spill the dirt to Mom and Dad about the other and not even begin to make up stories. The truth was always much more fun to expose.

Eliab for his part is simply exposing particular weaknesses he already sees in David. Why would he pull those two, pride and deceit, out of thin air? After all, isn't he right about David being the one who normally tends the sheep? Why would he be right about the sheep part but not about the character flaws? Why would he be wrong in seeing a tendency in a younger brother for pride and deceit? Even at this early juncture?

Is it not our families who know us best? Especially in the areas where we struggle? That is one of life's little realities. Living in close proximity with others brings out the best and the worst in everyone. And if anyone knows where our areas of struggle are, it is the very people we share a roof with.

So, I see no reason for Eliab to lie here. Besides, what would get more traction? Legitimate dirt on someone, or a fabrication that always holds the threat of being exposed as a lie. Personally, I'll take the dirt as leverage every time. True, Eliab may be bitter and jealous at the turn of events with David, but that in no way means he's resorting to making something up in a moment of confrontation.

Which is why I find this passage so intriguing. Again, we have this hint of something in David that has the potential to become something more. As we progress into his life, these hints from the biblical authors probe a life that is at once magnificent in its commitment to God, but human nevertheless. The evidence from David's life, is that we are often the most vulnerable immediately after a victory. When we begin to believe our own press, then we are ripe for a fall.

David is experiencing his star rising. As we've seen with many a young person who has ever had exposure to fame and fortune early on, the pressure of adulation and idolatry against the lack of maturity can cripple a life. For David, his conquest over Goliath and the prospect of reigning over a nation came quickly and early, experiences that for most of us rarely happen within an entire lifetime, let alone in the brief years of youth.

The wonder of Scripture rests in this very fact. The portraits of its heroes and saints are expressed in all its human dimensions. God, supreme and sovereign, remains the central figure and focus of the Bible. But the grandeur of God is not simply told in a purely didactic way where his characteristics are presented as a shopping list. They are told and celebrated in the lives of those who claim faith and do their best to live out that faith with integrity and purpose. As we continue to see, despite our best intentions and purpose of heart, we can sometimes become our own worst enemy and even commit the very blunders we endeavor to avoid.

Breakdown Dead Ahead

From the victory over Goliath, the life of David the warrior had begun. Regarding the years as Israel's second king, his prowess on the battlefield became legendary. He was fierce in battle and commanded the armies that were under him with courage and strength. Couple those accomplishments with David's musical skills and sensitivity and you have a man for all seasons. He easily garnered a nation's loyalty and love, as stated in 1 Samuel 18:16:

> But all Israel and Judah loved David because he was so successful at leading his troops into battle.

Further, he established himself as God's man. Beyond the adulation of his people, God greatly prospered David. At first glance, his appears to be a textbook case for the perfect life. But as mentioned above, the seeds that exist in David germinate throughout his life. There are moments when David becomes a victim of self-sufficiency, arrogance, and pride. Whenever he yielded to the passions of the flesh, David found himself in trouble.

As king, David indulged himself in every pleasure a man could want. Nothing was outside of his reach. Women, slaves, the allegiance of an army and a people. Tales of battles won and cities plundered. The gifting of a writer who could pen the Psalms and lull a former king to peace through song. With such accomplishments a person can become complacent and self-consumed, even beginning to see themselves as masters of their own destiny with nothing and no one to impede their progress.

Such is the danger of pride and arrogance, attributes that we see hints of in David's life-especially when David forgets the Lord and depends upon his own sufficiency. That's when trouble happens for most of us. When we experience difficulty it fosters in us a sense of dependency. But when everything is working in our favor, pride flourishes. It was an ever present hazard in David's life, but one story brings it to light above the rest.

In 1 Samuel 11, we enter into the darkest chapter of David's life. He is likely in his fifties and has been king some twenty years. It portrays one of his weakest moments, a stark contrast for a king who is known for his depth of character and courage. This lapse in judgement didn't happen overnight, though. The potential for such a fall had been percolating for some time. It begins innocently enough.

> In the spring of the year, when kings normally go out to war, David sent Joab and the Israelite army to fight the Ammonites. They destroyed the Ammonite army and laid siege to the city of Rabbah. However, David stayed behind in Jerusalem. (2 Samuel 11:1)

From the outset, we are told that David is where he should not have been. The writer wants us to recognize this. What's about to transpire could have been avoided *if David* was where he belonged, with his troops. Here, away from his responsibilities he is vulnerable while accountable to no one. The combination proves lethal.

> Late one afternoon, after his midday rest, David got out of bed and was walking on the roof of the palace. As he looked out over the city, he noticed a woman of unusual beauty taking a bath. (2 Samuel 11:1)

As we have stressed in previous passages, details in the text are important. The woman David observes is physically attractive beyond description. Her beauty is something you have got to see to believe, and when you do, your heart races from the sight. And apparently it did for David. The lure of temptation and desire overtake him to such degree that after he finds out who she is, he sends for her.

Let me linger here a moment. I'm imagining that anyone reading this story has experienced the lure of temptation. It has that ability to dampen our senses while heightening the need. It can fill us with such longing that all reason gets muted. The appetite that is piqued cannot be satisfied unless the need is fulfilled. God somehow vanishes from the scene. Our whole psyche is transfixed on a single purpose and anything else is needless distraction, even if it's a voice of reason. Time seems suspended and reality lost. And what's worse, the consequences of temptation are never really considered in the moment.

It doesn't take much imagination to recreate in your own mind what likely went through David's. Transfixed by the beauty bathing below, there is only one purpose in his mind, "Got to have her!" And have her he does. The text tells us that he gets exactly what his lust demanded. Far from this being David's only indiscretion, matters are about to get a whole lot worse.

The woman, Bathsheba, discovers that she is pregnant and sends word to David of her plight. Bathsheba is married to a man named Uriah, so instantly David conceives a plan to cover up his indiscretion. One night, one lapse in judgement, one moment of pleasure, and now a whole series of events follow that leave a trail of collateral damage. That's the reality when we yield to temptation. There is always collateral damage.

And Uriah will suffer greatly for something he had no part of. To complicate matters further he is no ordinary soldier, but held the designation as one of David's mighty men. A member of his elite guard who would be fearlessly loyal to the king and to his service, which makes David's treachery even more repulsive.

A situation that began badly now escalates quickly to worse. In an attempt to cover up the affair, David calls Uriah back from the battle lines in the hopes of hiding Bathsheba's pregnancy, fully expecting that Uriah will take advantage of this time to be with his wife. Instead, Uriah does the unexpected.

> But Uriah didn't go home. He slept that night at the palace entrance with the king's palace guard. When David heard that Uriah had not gone home, he summoned him and asked, "What's the matter? Why didn't you go home last night after being away for so long?" Uriah replied, "The Ark and the armies of Israel and Judah are living in tents, and Joab and my master's men are camping in the open fields. How could I go home to wine and dine and sleep with my wife? I swear that I would never do such a thing." (2 Samuel 11:9-11)

Don't you just hate it when a plan goes south because the person won't co-operate, primarily because he has more integrity than you? For all of David's machinations with Uriah, he can't get the guy to drop his guard and go sleep with his wife.

Instead, David gets exactly what he should get from a loyal member of his guard, a sense of duty to the men with which he serves. So much so that his conscience will not allow him even a night of pleasure as long as his comrades are roughing it on the battlefield.

David tries again to persuade Uriah, but he will have none of it. In desperation, David moves to Plan C and sends word to his commander, Joab, to place Uriah in the front of the battle where the fighting is fiercest. Unsettling is the fact that Uriah himself unknowingly carried the sealed letter to Joab which ordered him to put Uriah in harm's way.

So Joab assigned Uriah to a spot close to the city wall where he knew the enemy's strongest men were fighting. And when the enemy soldiers came out of the city to fight, Uriah the Hittite was killed along with several other Israelite soldiers. (2 Samuel 11:16-17)

The consequences of David's actions continue to multiply. Beyond the murder of Uriah, other soldiers paid with their lives as well. As we stated earlier, there is always collateral damage when we sin. And the greater the platform or responsibility we bear, the greater the consequences of that damage. Though Bathsheba becomes David's wife and a son is born, the chapter ends with this simple epitaph.

But the LORD was displeased with what David had done. (2 Samuel 11:27)

We can't displease God and get away with it. As the following chapter begins we are introduced to the prophet Nathan, whose confrontation brings a confession from David. Nathan has not only been tasked by God to confront the king, but also to pronounce upon him the consequences of his actions. The child would not survive.

Nathan, the prophet of the Lord, leads David to understand just how serious his mistake is. And in the aftermath of the event, as God causes David to lose a child as a consequence of his sin, David begins to take steps to put life back together for himself and Bathsheba.

Nonetheless, the prophet Nathan, beyond confronting David of his sin, leaves this dire prediction as a lingering consequence of his tryst with Bathsheba:

From this time on, your family will live by the sword because you have despised me by taking Uriah's wife to be your own. "This is what the LORD says: Because of what you have done, I will cause your own household to rebel against you. I will give your wives to another man before your very eyes, and he will go to bed with them in public view.

You did it secretly, but I will make this happen to you openly in the sight of all Israel." (2 Samuel 12:10-12)

What this means is that out of David's own house trouble will be a constant problem. David will live under persistent threat from his own family. And if you follow the story of David's kin from this point forward, the family is in classic dysfunction mode. Such are the dangers of pride and arrogance.

Repeat Offender

The consequences of a leader who wanders from God are far reaching. Though David was a godly man, there were times when he acted anything but. Before we close out this section I want to highlight one last story from David's life. Why this is important is because following the incident with Bathsheba, our assumption would be that David would be more diligent in guarding his heart from the Trojan Horse of pride. But this account taken later in his life, demonstrates that his struggles continue.

We all believe that with age comes the benefits of experience and wisdom. Age, we are led to believe, will keep us immune to the failures of the past. But some habits are hard to break and once again we find David in familiar territory.

In 2 Samuel 24, we read the account of David ordering Joab, the Commander of the army to take a census of Israel and Judah:

Once again the anger of the LORD burned against Israel, and he caused David to harm them by taking a census. "Go and count the people of Israel and Judah," the LORD told him. So the king said to Joab and the commanders of the army, "Take a census of all the tribes of Israel--from Dan in the north to Beersheba in the south--so I may know how many people there are." But Joab replied to the king, "May the LORD your

God let you live to see a hundred times as many people as there are now! But why, my lord the king, do you want to do this?" But the king insisted that they take the census, so Joab and the commanders of the army went out to count the people of Israel. (2 Samuel 24:1)

We are not told why the Lord was angry with the nation. Whatever the reason, it incites David to count the people. Joab, realizing the lack of wisdom in such a move challenges the king, but to no avail. For now, Joab does as he is told recognizing that the people would likely see it as a prelude to taxation or military service. Not necessarily a welcomed proposition by the populous.

David's motive was likely pride. To demand such an accounting for no reason likely meant that David wanted to know how big his kingdom and holdings were, the extent of his reach and the numbers that bowed to his authority and the vastness of those under his command.

It took a little over nine months for the census to be completed and when all was said and done verse 10 continues the story:

But after he had taken the census, David's conscience began to bother him. And he said to the LORD, "I have sinned greatly by taking this census. Please forgive my guilt, LORD, for doing this foolish thing." (2 Samuel 24:10)

David may have his weak moments, but one of the primary reasons he is characterized as a man after God's heart is seen here. Within David there is an acknowledgement of his sin and error before God. Beyond that, though, David comes to the Lord in forgiveness and repentance. He ties responsibility when he is wrong. David, who is answerable to no one, who could do and ask for whatever he wished, demonstrates the heart that God saw years ago when Samuel entered his home to anoint him as king.[1]

Despite his contrition, the Lord sends the prophet Gad to present David with the options for punishment. The lesson here is clear. Whenever we forget God by allowing pride, arrogance, or self-righteousness to get in the way, we limit our faith and open ourselves up to derailment. Secondly, even when we seek forgiveness and acknowledge our wrongs, it does not absolve us from the consequences of our actions.

In this particular case, David's indiscretion resulted in a plague that took the lives of 70,000 people. The sins of a leader invariably exact a high price. What I find most telling is the consequences relate to the initial sin. David's pride led him to want an inventory of his greatness, to put numbers to his accomplishments. Whatever pride was gained from the totals the census gave him, though, was now reduced by 70,000.

In similar fashion to the way God made Moses re-chisel the tablets of stone after he angrily destroyed the originals, David is told to build an altar for sacrifice and prayer. Without hesitation, a now contrite king builds, sacrifices, and prays, bringing the devastating plague to an end.

David's pride got in the way of his holiness and purity. Even at this late stage in his life. So for David, his tendency towards pride became his Trojan Horse. This man of God who otherwise lived in light of the Lord's precepts, allowed his faith to be compromised. Though greatly blessed by God, his arrogance from time to time elevated David above his Lord and in those brief moments allowed hubris to overtake holiness.

I have intentionally shaped this look at David's life from a very narrow framework. In order to show that even a great king like David is not immune to having his strengths undermined. The very qualities that propelled him to succeed also left him vulnerable, exposed, and weak. The writer of 1 Kings summarizes his life this way:

For David had done what was pleasing in the LORD's sight and had obeyed the LORD's commands throughout his life, except in the affair concerning Uriah the Hittite. (1 Kings 15:5)

Perhaps due to his propensity to fail from time to time, David's greatest legacy may lie elsewhere. For all of his achievements he also had great capacity for humility, contrition, and self reflection. When he comes to his senses and acknowledged his failure before God, his capacity for grief over his sin is one of the great gifts he leaves on the pages of the Bible.

David's words have resonated with many throughout history. I would venture to say that here is where David's greatness truly lies. In giving us the words of forgiveness, hope, and repentance, we have a language for those sorrowful moments when our own guilt, failures, and wounds are too deep. And because of them, David's words point us in the only direction that matters-heavenward, into the very throne room of God. The only one who is able take the brokenness of our lives and bring real healing and hope.

As we close this chapter, I want to leave you with a sampling of David's timeless words:

Oh, what joy for those whose disobedience is forgiven, whose sin is put out of sight! Yes, what joy for those whose record the LORD has cleared of guilt, whose lives are lived in complete honesty! When I refused to confess my sin, my body wasted away, and I groaned all day long. Day and night your hand of discipline was heavy on me. My strength evaporated like water in the summer heat. Finally, I confessed all my sins to you and stopped trying to hide my guilt. I said to myself, "I will confess my rebellion to the LORD." And you forgave me! All my guilt is gone. (Psalm 32:1-5)

CHAPTER 7

The Trojan Horse of Pride

"The proud person always wants to do the right thing, the great thing. But because he wants to do it in his own strength, he is fighting not with man, but with God." Søren Kierkegaard

I have a confession to make. There is one part of a funeral service that I actually look forward to. I know it may sound weird, but can you guess what it is? It's the eulogy, that part of the ceremony where loved ones, friends, and relatives get to share their favorite stories and memories.

Within thirty minutes to an hour, an entire life is summarized by a few anecdotes and reminiscences. The sum total of a life that encompassed school, work, relationships, victory, tragedy, accomplishments, and family. So much to tell in so little time. I've heard eulogies that were inspiring, and made me regret that I had not known the person better and I've heard others that made me weep, because little was said of any worth or value. Imagine coming to the end of your days and it all comes down to nothing more than an advertisement between programs.

With all the funerals I've been to (and I have been to a lot), rarely was the word pride not part of the eulogy. I've listened to how they had pride in their children, pride in their heritage, pride in their work, and even pride in their accomplishments. I've even heard less honorable achievements. Pride in their drinking ability, pride in their gambling streak, even pride in their many failed marriages.

There appears something anti-human about being pride-less. It just sounds wrong to have no affinity with anything close to your heart that makes you swell with pride about something in your life. Can you imagine for a moment a parent stating they had no pride in their children, a soldier with no pride in their country, or a scientist having no pride in their work? To hear such statements would signal that the person had experienced disappointment, disillusionment, or a loss of trust in the very place we would have expected some element of pride.

Pride is one of humanity's most celebrated characteristics yet it can be the most insidious of them all. For despite its endearing nature, pride has a dark side. We've all experienced that subtle shift that has us beaming one minute then looking down on someone else the next. What complicates it further is how blurred the line is between those moments when pride is serving us in a good way and when it's not.

The overwhelming evidence of the Bible treats pride as a dangerous commodity. Scant few verses treat it with any kind of positive press.[1] It's like having a tiger as a house pet. It may be cute when it's young, but the larger it grows, the more potentially dangerous it becomes. As far as the biblical writers are concerned, pride is best left in the shadows and make sure you never make a habit of feeding it.

All who fear the LORD will hate evil. Therefore, I hate pride and arrogance, corruption and perverse speech. (Proverbs 8:13)

This passage in Proverbs presents an interesting relationship. Those who have any affinity for God, who live in reverence of him, will have an aversion towards evil. But look at the "therefore," and what is defined as evil. Pride and arrogance top the list. These are pretty strong sentiments for a characteristic that we actively celebrate.

We are cautious to level anything as evil, a trend I personally find frightening. We are far more comfortable to label actions, even abhorrent ones, as expressions of some past injustice that pushed the person to act the way they did. But even without that cultural tension that exists with attaching the term evil to something, few would ever use it in the context of pride.

Learning to See It Clearly

I believe that perhaps the Bible is on to something. We've all been on the wrong end of someone's arrogance. In fact, our feelings of victimization are likely due to having become the objects of another's pride. Behind most prejudices is an attitude of either fear, hatred, or superiority. Regardless of reason, pride is an active participant. Whenever we've been given bragging rights, pride's been given permission to enter the game.

Arrogance and pride are ripe for feeding judgmental attitudes. Whatever allows us to feel a sense of superiority over another lends us to looking down on them. Our entire social structure is built on the "haves" and "have nots," and I couldn't in a million books elucidate the witness of history of the ever prominent "us" against "them." It has been a line of division in everything from politics to personal.

For those of us in the church world, the ugliest form of pride is our tendency to become self-righteous. This ailment diminishes our ability to be teachable and causes us to be openly judgmental. It's not only destructive in the way we are perceived by others, but we lose an openness to God moulding and shaping our life.

One of the most maligned groups in the New Testament are the Pharisees. This is interesting to note because if any believer living today were in first century Palestine in the time of Jesus they would likely belong to this group. But what is truly a lesson for us today is the way in which Jesus interacted with them. The harshest criticisms out of Jesus' mouth were directed at this group. He called them "white-washed tombs" and "hypocrites," among others things.

As much as I relish the way Jesus stood up to them it does hit close to home. Here is Jesus, in the midst of the most religious culture, whose reason for existence was a nation formed to be God's vehicle to the rest of the world, and yet they have become so arrogant that they were missing the heart of God. That is the danger of self-righteousness when we can look the part, act the part, speak the part, teach the part, and even get paid for the part, yet be distant from the most important part-a vital connection with God.

The more self-sufficient we become the less likely we need God. This is one of our culture's great disadvantages. The more we grow in our self-reliance the less we feel a need for God. Pride and arrogance feed into this in spades. Ever hear someone say, "I can take care of myself," "I don't need you," or my personal favorite, "only the weak need God." In my mind, these are nothing more than "pride proclamations!"

I think it is pretty obvious when we come across an arrogant person. You can see them coming from a mile away. They are one of the easiest animals to spot. What is it about them that makes them stand out like a peacock in full plumage? The answer is quite simple, actually. We all have a kind of sixth sense whenever we are in the presence of a person who cares only for themselves. Further, we also know that whatever relationship we have with the individual will be governed by rules that are meant to benefit them.

James Borg in his book, Persuasion, The Art of Influencing People, has a chapter on dealing with difficult people. One section specifically pertains to personality and how to identify and negotiate with the different types. He notes the "self-important" person and I like what he writes:

> We come across these people in the workplace and in everyday life. Generally they are only concerned about themselves. They don't even think they have to put themselves in another person's shoes. Consequently, they see the world only from their own perspective. You know this type-a condescending tone and body language that screams superiority. Ignore their arrogance (quite often it's a mask) and resolve not to let it get to you. Understand that they are looking for utterances from you that convey weakness that they can seize upon-so choose your words carefully and be sure of your facts.[2]

As you were reading that description how many people came to mind? They are in our lives everywhere. But the real problem is their ability to infect us. Just by living and breathing on this planet we are in danger of coming under the wiles of pride. If you have any ambition, any thought of success, any desire to make it to the top, or to become best in class at whatever, then pride will at some level be a partner in your life.

Unhealthy pride, by definition, is an excessively high opinion of oneself. This results in a person's needs, desires, reputation, dignity, and public persona being his or her main interest and concern, regardless of the effect on others. And as we saw in the last chapter, the evidence of pride can be found in the most contrite of hearts.

The downfall of many leaders is their early successes can begin to inflate their egos. We certainly saw this with David. Any leader who begins to see themselves as infallible or invincible will quickly dislodge themselves from reality. The trappings of power can lull anyone into a false sense of self worth. Ego can become a dangerous byproduct of a leader who holds himself above everyone else.

So any kind of drive toward success that focuses primarily on the externals without a desire to develop yourself internally is a recipe for derailment. At some point, one will overtake the other, and without the existence of strong moral character you will not be able to sufficiently hold onto the responsibilities that the success demands. There will be a convergence of strength over the weak areas of your life and the strengths will overwhelm.

Besides, most who want to succeed often engage in intense development of skills and expertise related to the field they want to succeed in. But few invest an equal amount of energy on developing their character and integrity. Over time, the character development can become outdistanced by the external success. The resulting void between success and the character to manage it, is where arrogance gains a foothold. And it's this disparity between the level of success against a person's character where many leaders fail.

The work of character building is arduous and time consuming but its benefits cannot be overstated. However, the ability to "power down" as your level of success and accomplishments grow will be one of the most important personal investments you can make. The Book of Proverbs states it well:

Pride goes before destruction, and haughtiness before a fall. (Proverbs 16:18)

Pride ends in humiliation, while humility brings honor. (Proverbs 29:23)

According to these passages, if you allow yourself to be governed by pride and arrogance you will eventually fail. You may not believe it now but it will catch up to you and it will take you down. I've seen it time and time again. I've born painful witness to it in my own life. The greatest failure in my life was a direct result of my own pride. To this day it still feels raw, even though years have passed. But that is the nature of pride. You can feed it, but you certainly can't beat it.

Pride will present you with a false image of the real you, one that forces you to live a lie. What's really crazy is everyone around you knows it, except you. And the longer you live that lie, the greater you lack the awareness of your true self. Without that self-awareness you will never be the kind of person who will make the world a better place.

The Way Forward

How then can we guard ourselves from pride or arrogance becoming a Trojan Horse? The answer has already been alluded to in one of the Proverbs quoted above. The way forward is to foster a life of humility. Let me back it up with another passage:

> And all of you, serve each other in humility, for "God opposes the proud but favors the humble." (1 Peter 5:5b)

Based on this text, you invoke resistance from God when you allow pride to rule your life. Now, be sure you grasp the weight of this passage. Our first impulse is to see this opposition from God as an act of judgement on His part. In truth, that would be the wrong way to understand it. In fact, if you take that posture it will evoke in you a tinge of pride and you will miss the full import of what is being said.

God knows us better than we know ourselves, and He knows the detrimental effects that pride can have in our lives. So, in knowing that, why would he encourage it? He really does care about you! And if you have any capacity to please God, then the path of pride is not going to do it. In fact, God will do His best to make sure it's a bumpy ride so you get the hint. Humility is the antidote to pride. God knows it, and the way to live a life that is favorable to God and a blessing to others is to seek humility.

We have an arresting passage about Jesus in Matthew 11:29:

> Take my yoke upon you. Let me teach you, because I am humble and gentle at heart, and you will find rest for your souls. (Matthew 11:29)

Remember in the previous chapter I stated that the Bible doesn't waste details just for text filler. This is another example. Of all the writings we have on Jesus, this is the only place where Jesus describes himself, where he gives personal details about the nature of his character. And notice that it's based on humility. Jesus not only wants to reveal a significant truth about his nature, but there is a lesson for us here as well. I cannot stress how important this principle of humility is. Let me press it further.

One of the most theologically profound passages in the entire Bible is found in chapter two of Philippians. The apostle Paul is writing to the church in Philippi in northern Greece and gives these words to them.

> Don't be selfish; don't try to impress others. Be humble, thinking of others as better than yourselves. Don't look out only for your own interests, but take an interest in others, too. You must have the same attitude that Christ Jesus had. Though he was God, he did not think of equality with God as something to cling to. Instead, he gave up his divine privileges; he took the humble position of a slave and was born as a human being. When he appeared in human form, he humbled himself in obedience to God and died a criminal's death on a cross. Therefore, God elevated him to the place of highest honor and gave him the name above all other names, that at the name of Jesus every

knee should bow, in heaven and on earth and under the earth, 11 and every tongue confess that Jesus Christ is Lord, to the glory of God the Father. (Philippians 2:3-10)

Notice the predominance of humility, especially as it relates to Jesus. He who was God (v. 6), came to earth, not as a king but as a slave, and even humbled himself in death. Wow, pretty profound. That the God of the universe, Creator Supreme, would send his Son for us. But here is what I want you to see for our purposes. The passage begins in verse 3 with an admonition for us to be humble! Look at verse 5. We need to have the same attitude as Jesus, the same Jesus who was God and came wrapped in human flesh to die for our sins!

As important as the passage is for theological reasons, its made more profound in that it serves as an illustration of the need to embrace humility. I find it incredibly challenging that one of the most important passages in the Bible in understanding Jesus was initiated by Paul's necessity to illustrate the importance of humility. And what better illustration than Jesus?

Let me make some additional remarks on humility. For many of us, we long for the world to be a better place. I believe the single greatest contribution you can make to the world is to invest in humility. Imagine for a moment if we all embraced it. How different would your marriage be? How different would the relationship with your kids, or in-laws, or parents be? What about your work? Would it make a difference on the national stage? Would it impact world hunger or world peace?

Humility, embraced by all, would dramatically alter the majority of our lives. Typically, humility is defined as an accurate self-assessment. It is a correct assessment of your strengths and as well as those areas you are weak, and living fully within that awareness. But how can we experience living with humility in practical ways?

I've found that in my years as a pastor, if I can give little action cues to help people begin to change unhealthy behaviours they are the most helpful. So when it comes to acting humble here is something that can become a verbal cue to get you pointed in the right direction. Humility will evidence itself most in those moments when you have the opportunity to exert power, but instead, choose to power down. Pride and arrogance promote a mentality of powering up, but humility powers us down.

When we power down we open ourselves up to being teachable, to accepting another's correction, to recognizing when we are wrong, to acknowledging we don't know everything, and it fosters our need for God. I would even venture to say that humility is an important ingredient to the long term health and survival of the human species.

It does not mean you stop making the hard decisions or command authority over situations. But it does shape *how* you do it. Most people recognize leadership done with humility as compared to those who live under a power model.

More Than a Feeling

Embracing humility can be intimidating. For some it may leave you feeling vulnerable at first. For others it may mean releasing your sense of power. The variables for each of us are different. You may at this juncture just hold this as a religious teaching with visions of monks humming in unison and not give it the weight it deserves. And if you are a leader in your organization, why is this particularly important for you? Let me give you more to chew on.

In his seminal work, *Good to Great*, Jim Collins researched the companies that made the leap to great and the distinctions that put them above the others. The successful leaders who stood above the rest were characterized by a paradoxical combination of extreme personal humility and intense professional will.[3]

106

Though the successful leaders demonstrated a fierce resolve and determination to see their organizations succeed, the personal characteristics of those same leaders were summarized as humble. Collins goes on to say:

> "Those who worked with or wrote about the good-to-great leaders continually used words like quiet, humble, modest, reserved, shy, gracious, mild-mannered, self-effacing, understated, did not believe his own clippings[4]"

The findings were somewhat surprising. Here at the helm of companies that were paragons of industry were individuals of humility where arrogance would have been anticipated. Especially with all the perceived trappings of success that would be evident in the environments of these organizations.

Let's be clear here about these findings. There are countless leaders in countless organizations who demonstrate a tireless commitment to their successes. The key variable in Collins's findings is in the personal nature of its leader. There are many good companies spread across the entire planet, but the great ones are lead by people of humility.

Tim Irwin has studied catastrophic failures of leadership and documented his findings in his book, *Derailed*. As he recounts the failures of six high profile leaders, he documents the commonalities of each. One of his key findings was a lack of humility.

> In my research of the highly placed leaders I profiled earlier in the book, it became apparent that arrogance was a key contributor to their derailments. If humility is having an accurate self-image and being other-oriented, then arrogance is its mirror opposite. Each executive profiled manifested this debilitating quality...that arrogance is

most often seen in the form of self-promotion and entitlement. Most derailed executives believed "a particular job was owed to them."[5]

If there is one thing that causes leaders to lose their ability to lead effectively, it's pride. It's at the core of many leadership failures. These failures reinforce the importance of humility in leaders. Notice in the citation from Irwin that a sense of entitlement becomes part of an arrogant leader. It becomes virtually impossible to create an environment of team work and common purpose when the motivation of a leader is getting what he needs at the expense of everyone else.

We've all met those leaders who are more interested in powering up. And as we stated earlier, pride and arrogance will bring you down and the fall will not be pleasant. More and more publications for business are recognizing that talent alone does not make a competent leader. It's a formula for inciting pride. Because of this growing awareness there is a resurgence of a little used word that's making a comeback in the business literature. The word is hubris and it dates back to Ancient Greece. It's a word that defines excessive pride that brings down a hero.[6]

Collins uses the term in his book, *How the Mighty Fall*, as a description of the initial stage of a company that is beginning to enter a death spiral. He identifies five stages that organizations progress through on the road to decline and irrelevance.

Collins gives his assessment of what happens in an organization when it enters the first stage of demise which he titles, Hubris Born of Success:

Great enterprises can become insulated by success; accumulated momentum can carry an enterprise forward, for a while, even if its leaders make poor decisions or lose discipline. Stage 1 kicks in when people become arrogant, regarding success virtually as an entitlement, and they lose sight of the true underlying factors that created success in the first place.[7]

Collins goes on to write that when the rhetoric of success focuses on the how, "We succeed because we do these things," rather than on the why, "We understand why we succeed and under what conditions it would no longer work," decline is likely to follow.[8] For leaders the propensity we have to settle in after a period of success is a dangerous lull to allow. As we've seen in the life of David, we are most vulnerable following a great victory.

Engaging in a posture of humility forces the why question to remain in the foreground. It serves as a caution against allowing success to fill your head and to dislodge your critical skills. Nothing is more damning than a leader, who is inflated by prior success, entering into auto-pilot mode. Decisions become reckless and ill-conceived while at the same time any questioning of their logic is treated like an act of treason.

One of the most telling signs that a leader has entered the space of hubris is when they no longer listen to opposing views or counter arguments. And let's face it, regardless of the type of organization you lead, making decisions is one of the primary tasks of a leader. The moment that becomes compromised is certainly one of the warning signs we should pay close attention to.

Making the Changes that Matter

In their book, *Decisive*, authors Chip and Dan Heath tackle this very vexing subject. The art of good decision making is critical for every leader. In truth, even on a personal level the decisions we make are what propel us on the paths we are currently on. It would be fair to say that your life right now is the sum total of the decisions you've made to date. So, when decisions on a personal level hold so much weight, how much more so will a decision in the mind of a leader that will affect many.

One of the studies they cite is the acquisitions that CEO's make that rarely pay off.[9] Two researchers, Hayward and Hambrick, analyzed every large acquisition conducted in public markets over a two-year period that were $100 million dollars or more. It totalled 106 transactions. They wanted to know if the price paid by the executives in the acquisitions was influenced by three things:

- Praise by the media
- Strong recent performance (which the CEO could interpret as evidence of their genius)
- A sense of self-importance

What the researchers were trying to determine was whether these factors tended to inflate the ego of the acquiring CEO and what effect it would have on the cost of the acquisition. What they found was that their suspicions were right in all three of their survey criteria. CEOs who "come to believe their own press, would end up paying extremely large acquisition premiums." In other words, the price a leader would offer in an acquisition would become inflated simply by their own hubris. Conversely, the researchers found that those CEOs who had people around them who could openly challenge their thinking were more likely to pay lower acquisition premiums.[10]

Humility, therefore, is a vital ingredient for a leader. Pride, arrogance, hubris, will eventually lead you to ultimately coming off the rails. What is common throughout our study of David and the research from Collins, Irwin, and the Heath brothers is that most of the leaders involved are intelligent, hard-working, committed, and highly motivated people. But time and again, these strengths do not always guarantee long term success or protection from eventual failure.

And in every study, a case can be made for the more successful leaders being the humble ones, those who have the capacity to power down, especially in those key situations when a weaker leader is trying to power up. To conclude this section, I want to give you some practical steps in guarding yourself from the dangers of pride, arrogance, and hubris, characteristics that I hope have shown to be hazardous to a leader's strengths.[11]

- Practice powering down. This does not mean that you become a door mat or that you relinquish your position or diminish your organization's mission or vision. It is a self-evaluation that causes you to recognize those moments when you are feeling superior, more capable, invincible, or untouchable. It alerts you when self-promotion overtakes the good of the organization or the people you lead.

- Make yourself accountable. Don't allow the press to become your gauge for success. Further, give the person the freedom to let you know when you are being over-confident, dismissive, over-bearing, and so forth. This is one way to keep you from the need to be greater than you are.

- Learn to listen to others. Yours is not the only opinion or perspective that matters. I believe that a leader's two great enemies are the people's perception and expectations of them. One of the more effective ways of curtailing the way people view you and what they expect from you is to be open to listening to them. This also gives you the ability to identify with others.

- Lastly, remember that the best leaders are the ones who serve others, not themselves. To be a leader is an awesome privilege. This principle is key for any leader who truly wants to affect their environment with positive change. Consider Jesus Christ. He is the consummate level 5 leader that Collins describes in *Good to Great*. He demonstrated a fierce resolve for the mission while maintaining a life of humility and service. Though his life was short, his example and teachings have affected the entire world for over 2000 years.

Pride can potentially become a Trojan Horse, and anytime you allow pride to diminish your capacity to lead from your strengths, it undermines your ability to lead well, or to lead at all.

CHAPTER 8

Intellectual Suicide

So King Solomon became richer and wiser than any other king on earth. (1 Kings 10:23)

The name most associated with the Law and Ten Commandments is Moses. If it's the Psalms the primary figure is David. But when it comes to the literature in the Bible known as wisdom, Solomon's your man.

In the years teaching the Wisdom Books, my students invariably come upon a dilemma, one to which I devote an entire lecture. Any time spent studying the life of Solomon causes the same question to arise: "How did the man that the Bible calls the wisest of his time end up so badly?"

It does cause one to wonder why the label doesn't match the life, at least by the time Solomon is old and grey. What is even more disturbing is that his life actually begins better than it ends. At least in terms of the decisions he makes. It borders on the unbelievable that a man endowed with wisdom would allow his life to take the direction that it does.

Therefore Solomon is one of the best figures in the entire Bible for demonstrating the premise of this book. The very strengths you possess can become the very vehicles for failure. In regard to Solomon, many believers don't know how to compensate for the inconsistency of his life. Especially since so much of the material ascribed to him ends up as some of our favorite verses for mounting on plaques and monuments. What he wrote may reflect wisdom, but how he lived it out is another matter entirely.

Rabbinical literature attributes the writings of Proverbs, Ecclesiastes, and the Song of Songs as representing the three stages of his life. "When a man is young he composes songs; when he grows older he makes sententious remarks; and when he becomes an old man he speaks of the vanity of things."[1]

The statement neatly packages the seasons of Solomon's life. If true, it is disturbing to me that the waning years of his life are the most conflicted with respect to God. He grows more detached from the things of God, and even borders on hopelessness. Striking when you consider that God was the one who gifted him with wisdom in the first place.

The Ultimate Gift

Born into privilege as the second son of King David and Bathsheba, Solomon became Israel's third king whose reign lasted some forty years. David's final instructions to his son were to encourage him to follow the Lord. Subsequent to David's death and his placement on the throne, Solomon is visited by God at an early age. Out of that visitation Solomon pleases God by his request for wisdom, not for wealth or power, which is what lesser men would have asked for. In response, God invokes a blessing upon Solomon's life that will encompass those things he did not ask for, because to have wisdom, is to have it all.

In the realm of faith, this is akin to winning the lottery. A young king in the early stages of his monarchy is approached by God in a dream. As if that wouldn't jolt you awake, God gives Solomon a proposition. "Ask me for anything and I will give it to you!" Imagine for a moment if you were given a virtual blank check from God. A gift of anything? What would you ask for?

Solomon, in a surprising demonstration of humility asks for the ability to discern right from wrong. Here is the way it reads in 1 Kings 3:7-14:

"Now, O LORD my God, you have made me king instead of my father, David, but I am like a little child who doesn't know his way around. And here I am in the midst of your own chosen people, a nation so great and numerous they cannot be counted! Give me an understanding heart so that I can govern your people well and know the difference between right and wrong. For who by himself is able to govern this great people of yours?" The Lord was pleased that Solomon had asked for wisdom. So God replied, "Because you have asked for wisdom in governing my people with justice and have not asked for a long life or wealth or the death of your enemies--I will give you what you asked for! I will give you a wise and understanding heart such as no one else has had or ever will have! And I will also give you what you did not ask for--riches and fame! No other king in all the world will be compared to you for the rest of your life! 14 And if you follow me and obey my decrees and my commands as your father, David, did, I will give you a long life."

God gives Solomon an incredible gift, beyond what he's really asked for. But notice in the passage something that often gets missed. It's in verse 14 and it's that little preposition, "if." Often when we read passages like this we are so taken by the promise that we miss the fact that it is conditional. It's like signing a contract but never reading the fine print.

God has not granted this gift to Solomon carte blanche. It comes with a condition that Solomon will be faithful in the same way that David was. As believers we often embrace the promises of God as if they belong to us without question. But many demand obedience, because obedience precedes blessing. And it is no different for Solomon, even though God has looked upon him with incredible favor.

Secondly, and this is doubly important to grasp, a gift like this from God is meant for His purposes. That is primarily why they are given in the first place. But often we treat these gifts and abilities as vehicles for our own advancement and procure the favor of others, rather than the favor of God. We get to use them and benefit from them yes, but ultimately they are meant for God's purposes and glory.

There is also a prior condition that was imposed on every king that reigned over Israel and Judah, one that essentially was broken by every king. Several hundred years earlier, Moses pens the Book of Deuteronomy. The nation of Israel is perched on the border of the Promised Land preparing to enter. Moses, in leaving them final instructions, gives them the criteria for whenever they are ready to install a king. Remember, this is several hundred years before the time of Solomon. This is what we read:

> You are about to enter the land the LORD your God is giving you. When you take it over and settle there, you may think, 'We should select a king to rule over us like the other nations around us.' If this happens, be sure to select as king the man the LORD your God chooses. You must appoint a fellow Israelite; he may not be a foreigner. "The king must not build up a large stable of horses for himself or send his people to Egypt to buy horses, for the LORD has told you, 'You must never return to Egypt.' The king must not take many wives for himself, because they will turn his heart away from the LORD. And he must not accumulate large amounts of wealth in silver and gold for himself. "When he sits on the throne as king, he must copy for himself this body of instruction on a scroll in the presence of the Levitical priests. He must always keep that copy with him and read it daily as long as he lives. That way he will learn to fear the LORD his God by

obeying all the terms of these instructions and decrees. This regular reading will prevent him from becoming proud and acting as if he is above his fellow citizens. It will also prevent him from turning away from these commands in the smallest way. And it will ensure that he and his descendants will reign for many generations in Israel. (Deuteronomy 17:14-20)

Long before the Israelites established themselves in the land, Moses laid out the requirements for a king. Remember, nowhere do we find anything that states that this passage from Moses no longer applies. Yet, Solomon broke virtually every stipulation. The actions of Solomon, as well as David before him, treat the passage as if it doesn't pertain to them.

Though David made allegiances, became wealthy, and had many wives and concubines, these pale in comparison to the extravagances of Solomon. One of the first things Solomon did when he was firmly established as king was make an alliance with Egypt and marry one of the Pharaoh's daughters. Strike one. Over the course of his lifetime he took many wives and concubines. In fact, I Kings 11:3 says he had 700 wives and 300 concubines. Strike two.

He added wealth, built elaborate stables, and the list goes on. Strike three, four,…etc. And if you were able to ask Solomon about the requirements of Moses he likely would answer they were not applicable to the present reality. Moses wrote at a time where he couldn't have known what lay ahead for the nation. After-all, the present political climate demanded that a king forge allegiances through marriage. A king would need to acquire resources for the sake of the kingdom and for the welfare of the people. There are certain trading partners critical for commerce so we must adjust the way we conduct ourselves.

The reasons for justifying the disregard of the earlier passage are many. But regardless, they ignore a set of stipulations that in God's eyes, continue to have force. And we can be guilty of the same. Have you ever thought a passage irrelevant for our time? How many situations do we justify because the attitude is that we have evolved. We live in a modern world and the times have changed. What was right for them can't apply to us because we're smarter and understand the world much better.

Garbage in Leads to Garbage Out

It's easy to fall into that trap, mostly because, like Solomon, we can be very good at lying to ourselves. For Solomon, who was known for his wisdom, the temptation to begin believing his own press would have been daunting to resist. Over time, he would enjoy more riches, more women, more prestige-the cycle would escalate without restraint.

How long would it have taken before he began to believe in his own infallibility? Solomon had everything a man could want and more. And by all accounts, he enjoyed having it too. And this is where the heart of Solomon's failure rests. Before we get there, though, I want to highlight some of Solomon's own writings. The Bible tells us that he enjoyed collecting wisdom sayings, so he was immersed in literature that was meant to teach wise living. This one is a favorite:

Guard your heart above all else, for it determines the course of your life. (Proverbs 4:23)

There is one piece of advice that Solomon neglected and it's taught in this verse. If there is a grand failure that Solomon is guilty of it's not guarding his own heart. There was an axiom in the early days of computers that taught, "garbage in, garbage out." Whatever we expose our hearts to can have the potential of steering the course for the rest of our lives.

In the Bible the word heart has a broader meaning than it does in our contemporary culture. We tend to separate the mind and the heart, but for the ancients the mind and the heart were more intimately related, almost synonymous. Thus, the point of this passage is that whatever you think, comes out in your actions and in the way you perceive yourself. And if you are thinking wrongly, you will end up experiencing wrong emotions, reacting wrongly in situations, and demonstrating wrong behaviour, which ultimately leads to a life of struggle and unhappiness.

Solomon, though considered a wise man, fell into the trap of pride and arrogance which caused him to become over-confident, leaving his heart unguarded and unprotected. But his lack of diligence was a byproduct of his gift of wisdom. The very notion that you possess extraordinary mental prowess, would likely lull you into believing that you could manage your way out of situations that other less intelligent people could not. Especially if, over time, you allowed arrogance to lure you into believing that God was no longer your master. A lack of accountability on a human level eventually transforms itself to a lack of accountability to God.

This is a prevalent pattern today. The more we believe in our own wisdom the more we tend to drift from God. This is evident in the ongoing tension between faith and science. I'm fascinated they have become a battleground, rather than complimentary disciplines. For many, science has become nothing more than a convenient vehicle for discarding God. Unfortunately, science has become one of the more blatant forms of idolatry today, elevating it above the need for a Creator.

One of the great barriers to wisdom is pride. And just because God gave Solomon the gift of wisdom doesn't mean he removed the potential for pride. Regardless of what we are entrusted with by God, the expectations are always that our dependency will be on him and not ourselves. That is the danger of pride, it has the subtle propensity to shift the dependency from God to ourselves. These warnings are evident throughout the wisdom literature. The very writings attributed to Solomon himself.

> Pride leads to disgrace, but with humility comes wisdom. (Proverbs 11:2)

We've talked about pride and arrogance in the previous two chapters but unfortunately it rears its ugly head in the life of Solomon too. But unlike his father David, Solomon's failure manifested itself differently. Sadly, he did not demonstrate a contrite and repentant heart like his father. Something to which his wisdom may have actually acted as a barrier. Solomon's own perception of himself may have kept him from believing that he needed to repent. With the passing of time, his own sense of infallibility may have hardened him from seeing the need.

> Pride goes before destruction, and haughtiness before a fall. (Proverbs 16:18)

You can believe all the press about yourself, but eventually it will catch up with you. The legacy of fallen leaders is a testament to the perils of pride, but it's a vixen that's hard to divorce. Therefore, one of the great barriers to wisdom is pride, which then creates a barrier to God.

> Fear of the LORD is the foundation of wisdom. Knowledge of the Holy One results in good judgment. (Proverbs 9:10)

From the standpoint of the biblical literature, wisdom begins with the recognition of who God is. God is the source of all wisdom, and wisdom begins by properly aligning ourselves with who he is. Proper recognition results in reverence (i.e., the fear of the Lord) that lends itself to a life of submission and obedience. This goes to demonstrate that one of the primary theological notions of the wisdom literature is rooted in the idea of humility. Something that a wise man like Solomon should have understood.

Two Lures that Catch Us All

Let's clear the air for a moment. Solomon's accomplishments were many and he achieved feats befitting a king. His wisdom was celebrated and demonstrated in stories such as the visit of the Queen of Sheba in 1 Kings 10. In fact, the Queen confirmed that the gossip concerning the depth of his wisdom was beyond what she heard (vs. 7). From the standpoint of his ability to govern, his wisdom was credited for his diplomacy, building projects, commerce, and administration.

Solomon becomes the principle architect that God uses to build the Temple in Jerusalem, something that God denied David because he had too much blood on his hands. His capacity for amassing vast amounts of knowledge is coupled with the deposit he makes in the books of Proverbs, Ecclesiastes, and Song of Songs. He was the proverbial rock star of his day.[2]

Which is the natural way of things. We all have gifts, talents, and abilities that help us make positive contributions to the world around us. Solomon was no different other than the platform he enjoyed as king. So, with all that he had at his disposal, what went wrong?

It's a common refrain in our time. Even in the church world I've witnessed some of the most tragic failures by some of the most talented people. One leader I admired when I first entered ministry crashed in a spectacular fireball. This at a time when the church was exploding and his star was rising faster than you can imagine. Though it has been many years now, the fallout and wounds have never really left the church.

Solomon was very good at lying to himself. Actually, we all are. We are very good at convincing ourselves of what we really want to hear, even when we know it's wrong. We can even sense in our gut that it may end badly, but we still fool ourselves into believing that whatever the consequences we'll be able to manage them.

For most the two biggest purchases we make are our homes and cars. Even with these major financial decisions, emotions play a major role in what we buy. How many have stretched their budget beyond their agreed limit the minute they saw the kitchen of their dreams or sat in that red two-seater that brought thoughts of younger days.

That's a tug we've all felt. But what really caused Solomon to fall was the sin of infidelity. Remember how we said the Solomon did not guard his heart? Whenever you leave it exposed you leave yourself open to the potential of infidelity. Also, the passage said to "guard" your heart which stresses the need to actively put safeguards in place that protect you from the potential for infidelity. Consider it a type of firewall for the heart.

I want to take us back to the passage we pulled from Deuteronomy that Moses wrote as a template for future Israelite kings. There is one piece, the first part of verse 17 that is the key to the epic fail of Solomon. Here it is again.

The king must not take many wives for himself, because they will turn his heart away from the LORD. (Deuteronomy 17:17a)

In the Hebrew, this passage is structured as a command, similar to the way the Ten Commandments are. Their force stress the importance of adhering to the precepts it demands. This one command was a great struggle for Solomon. It became his blind spot.

That's what happens with pride. It can create a blind spot in us. What can be disturbing is our strengths can become the blind spot itself. It's akin to a mother's love that is so consumed with caring for her children that she creates hyper-dependant kids who cannot function in the real world.

Which is why the antidote for pride is humility. Humility allows us to self-evaluate authentically and keeps us accountable to others. We rarely see the depth of our own blind spots, but they are often glaring signposts to others.

There are warnings the Bible gives from beginning to end. They are the warnings against temptation and idolatry-two partners in crime. The passage above speaks not only to both but also shows their relationship, because what tempts us physically will invariably tempt us spiritually.

The infidelity of Solomon is much deeper than simply the number of wives and mistresses he accumulated. His infidelity smacked against everything God had required of him. What may have seemed a necessity at first in order to form allegiances and such, was the very practice God cautioned against.

The continual warnings concerning temptation and idolatry need to be heeded. No one is immune to their allure. They are a part of the human experience that make up the majority of the Bible's cautionary passages.

A Two-Headed Dragon

Everyone is subject to temptation. It's how we respond to it that makes all the difference. No human has ever lived a life who hasn't felt the pull of temptation. Even Jesus experienced it, though he never gave in to it. Such is not the case for the rest of us. Remember the passage that cautioned us to "guard our heart?" I like how James frames this:

Temptation comes from our own desires, which entice us and drag us away. (James 1:14)

Temptation is a situation or circumstance that puts us to the test. It acts as a lure or trap that entices us into something that is sinful. Temptation is a threat, one with the potential to do great damage. That is the biblical distinction. In common culture, not so much. In fact we've made the allure of being tempted into a sport. Yet time and again, succumbing to temptation has consequences. Always, whether you are a believer or not, the aftermath of such actions is painful. We've just learned to numb ourselves of the reality.

Temptation for the most part is felt physically and emotionally. It's what we experience on a human level. It's an act of infidelity between one or more individuals. Solomon is guilty of infidelity because as king, the command was not to have many wives. Now I'm not going to argue if "many" wives in the text left any room for more than one, that's a silly argument based on the pattern set out in Genesis, but I can be pretty confident that 700 wives is way, way over the limit.[3]

Idolatry is likewise an ongoing vice we continue to struggle with as a society. Many treat idolatry as an ancient practice that consisted of bowing down to wooden images. Few would acknowledge idolatry as a modern problem that needs ancient wisdom and truth to counter its present effects.

An idol is any created thing that you expect will give you what only God can give you. The fact of the matter is that over time, our idols have become more subtle and evolved, but just as damning. Idols come in all shapes and sizes and can be personal, religious, cultural, or natural. We will deal with this in the next chapter but for now, the matter of idolatry was a huge problem for Solomon.

Because Solomon was tempted with many wives, he became

tempted to commit idolatry, which is the very warning given in the passage above. One will eventually lead to the other. Committing infidelity in the physical realm will lead to infidelity in the spiritual realm. Read the passage again:

> The king must not take many wives for himself, because they will turn his heart away from the LORD. (Deuteronomy 17:17a)

Because he did not "guard" his heart and yielded to temptation with many wives, they turned his heart away from God! Temptation will lead to idolatry because whenever you do not guard your heart you will allow anything to direct it. Before you know it you've allowed substantial distance to be placed between you and God. And depending on the length of time and the depth of the void, you can fool yourself into believing you no longer need God.

So infidelity happens on two planes. First, the horizontal, which is human to human, and secondly, the vertical, human to God. Both forms of infidelity hurt relationships and have dire consequences. We all know individuals who are victims of both these types of infidelity. The pain and hurt is real and palpable. From broken marriages and homes, to loved ones we grieve for because they've walked away from God altogether.

And both forms of infidelity are the focus of continual warnings in the Bible. The admonitions to flee from temptation and from idolatry are meant to help us guard our hearts. When we commit infidelity through temptation, we are distorting God's original intent for relationships. When we commit infidelity through idolatry, we are replacing our need for God with created things that will one day fade away, because only God can give us true meaning, value, and purpose.

The failures of Solomon are not based on conjecture or guesswork. The Bible is clear about what ensnared him. Don't imagine as you read his story that it happened overnight. Like most failures, it came gradually. That is where the danger lies.

I told you in the last chapter that I'm intrigued by eulogies. Some of the more fascinating ones come right out of the pages of Scripture. That is what we get with Solomon. In 1 Kings 11:1-13, we hear God's critique of the man who was granted wisdom beyond anyone else on the face of the earth. And yet, at the end of his days, here is what can be said of him by God. I've put in bold the verses of note:

Now King Solomon loved many foreign women. Besides Pharaoh's daughter, he married women from Moab, Ammon, Edom, Sidon, and from among the Hittites. **The LORD had clearly instructed the people of Israel, 'You must not marry them, because they will turn your hearts to their gods.' Yet Solomon insisted on loving them anyway.** He had 700 wives of royal birth and 300 concubines. **And in fact, they did turn his heart away from the LORD. In Solomon's old age, they turned his heart to worship other gods instead of being completely faithful to the LORD his God, as his father, David, had been.** Solomon worshiped Ashtoreth, the goddess of the Sidonians, and Molech, the detestable god of the Ammonites. **In this way, Solomon did what was evil in the LORD's sight; he refused to follow the LORD completely, as his father, David, had done.** On the Mount of Olives, east of Jerusalem, he even built a pagan shrine for Chemosh, the detestable god of Moab, and another for Molech, the detestable god of the Ammonites. **Solomon built such shrines for all his foreign wives to use for burning incense and sacrificing to their gods. The LORD was very angry with Solomon, for his heart had turned away from the LORD, the God of Israel, who had appeared to him twice. He had warned Solomon specifically about worshiping other gods, but Solomon did not listen to the LORD's command.** So now the LORD said to him, "Since you have not kept my covenant and have disobeyed my decrees, I will surely tear the kingdom away from you and give it to one of your servants. *But for the sake of your father, David, I will not do this while you are still alive. I will take the kingdom away from your son. And even so, I will not take away the entire kingdom; I will let him be king of one tribe, for the sake of my servant David and for the sake of Jerusalem, my chosen city.*" (1 Kings 11:1-13)

That is quite a eulogy. I've italicized the last two verses. Notice the incredible grace and patience of God. Despite the ongoing failures of Solomon, God keeps his promise, one that was made to his father David. Even in these moments when history has weighed in on the life of Solomon, God continues to keep his word and move his plan forward.

It is a characteristic of God we should never forget. Ever wondered about the risks God takes whenever he makes a promise that entails fallible creatures. The God of perfect knowledge and pure intentions striking up a partnership with people known for their tendency to wander. Look at the life of Solomon: He's given the gift of wisdom by God, and yet commits infidelity of the worse kind, gifts that were given with conditions and for the glory of God.

I want to close with some familiar verses. Maybe you've heard them, maybe they're new. My hope is that after this chapter, you will see them with new eyes.

Trust in the LORD with all your heart; do not depend on your own understanding. Seek his will in all you do, and he will show you which path to take. Don't be impressed with your own wisdom. Instead, fear the LORD and turn away from evil. (Proverbs 3:5-7)

CHAPTER 9

The Trojan Horse of Infidelity

"The Old Testament says that if God's people turn away in spiritual adultery, it will not be long until the following generations are engaged in physical adultery, for the two things go hand in hand . . . . Our generation proves this with overwhelming force. Let there be spiritual adultery and it will not be long until physical adultery sprouts like toadstools in the land. In the 1930s liberalism took over almost all the churches in the United States, and in the 1960s our generation is sick with promiscuous sex. It is the same in Britain and other countries. These things are not unrelated; they are cause and effect." Francis A. Schaeffer

I can still remember it. Maybe not every detail, but I can remember how it felt. It was alive, energetic, and inspiring. It was one of the few times that I was engaged from start to finish. The atmosphere was electric and the people, well, they were actually bearable. That had to count for something.

As a former musician I am very critical of music, so I can't tell you how thrilled I was to have found a team that could keep me engaged. I can still recollect the synchronization of each musician, the balance of their sound and the voices that were a pleasure to the ears. With each song you could tell that the music was more important than the egos of its members and it clearly showed.

Then came the speaker. Young, articulate, hadn't heard anyone quite like him before. Somehow he was able to speak candidly about the things that mattered and present them in a way that resonated with everyone. In fact, many years later I can say that he was the first person who taught me a few tricks on how to dynamically present in front of a crowd.

Yeah, I'm talking about church. My wife, Darlene and I, were preparing for our next ministry assignment and found a church that became our home in the interim. I can't tell you the impact that church had on my overall outlook. When I became a believer in my mid-twenties I was a recovering musician. I'll never forget my very first church experience. The language was from the 1600s, the music was nail scraping, and the dress was from the 60's. I was so dumbfounded that I kept looking around thinking we were on the set of one of those shows. You know, where they pop out and yell, "Just Kidding!" But nope, if this was staged it was the best group of actors I'd ever met. Imagine my surprise when I realized this was the real deal.

My relief at finding a church that was awake to its present reality was beyond words. It showed me that there were ministries that could bridge the culture gap and bring meaningful content into people's lives. They were growing like wildfire and it was an exciting community to be a part of.

Darlene and I ended up becoming involved in a minor leadership role. It felt right and it was helping us prepare for the next phase of our lives. The future could not have looked brighter. So imagine my surprise when I received a call at home informing me that the pastor had been caught in an affair. Not only that, but it was with a female staff member and the tryst had been going on for some time.

I don't know if you've ever had news that knocked the wind out of you. To say I was shocked is an understatement. What was tragic to watch was not only the demise of an exciting ministry, but more importantly, the devastation it left in their families. Spouses, children, relatives, the pain was evident everywhere.

I remember the fallout from the congregation, too. The people left to pick up the pieces, mostly the Board, did their best to bring a hurting community together and provide some direction. I have to confess that this was not only a very discouraging time but quite a frustrating time as well. I watched and listened as people made accusations and pointed blame. In one meeting, a member stood up and blamed the entire mess on the new-fangled music. Talk about being totally disconnected from reality. It took every ounce of restraint I could muster not to explode.

Many lives got derailed because of the indiscretion of two people. In particular the pastor who had an amazing future ahead of him and even today consider one of the best communicators I've ever heard. Now, almost two decades later, the church has yet to experience the kind of growth or energy since.

One last thought. I've had lots of time to mull over that particular situation, as well as talk with a number of the leaders. One note of interest was the growing uneasiness we were feeling about the pastor. In hindsight, there were a number of times when I was with him where I felt a surge of arrogance that didn't quite settle right. But as with all matters like this, I put aside the feeling, thinking it was over-reaction.

The Battle We're All Fighting!

That scenario, and many like it, have played out in countless churches. But it's not limited to the church world by any means. Whether at home, work, within government, or the military, you name it, the pain of infidelity has affected every strata of human existence.

In fact, from my viewpoint, it has become so common place that we've begun to numb ourselves to its affects. And when we numb ourselves from the fallout, we end up creating a culture that does not inform the next generation of the potential hazards awaiting them, and the spiral of numb lives continues. To be honest, I had a whole list of real life stories that I was wrestling with to use as an opening illustration for this chapter. The prevalence of these types of stories are a disturbing trend that does not seem to be abating anytime soon.

As stated earlier, there are two areas that the Bible warns us against continually-being tempted, and falling for idols. To take a step back further, pride and arrogance are characteristics that lend themselves to falling for temptation and worshipping idols. That's why as a leader, the importance of guarding your heart from these ailments is indispensable for the health of your organization.

Too many vital, growing, and important causes have been derailed because a dynamic leader became more enamoured with their own power and need satisfaction. Here is the fact of the matter: Regardless of the title you hold, the size of the organization you lead, or the accolades that you can claim, the most important person you will ever lead is yourself.

To put it more bluntly, true leaders have a fire within them. They long to change the world, to make it a better place, and to bring the changes needed for that reality to exist. Most leaders who can inspire and encourage have this innate burning within them. You can feel the heat if ever you get close enough. That is nowhere truer than for church leaders. Armed with the Gospel, the prospect of transforming people's lives becomes the sole focus for our existence and purpose.

Yet there is a subtle battle that gets fought, one that we've all felt and one that keeps pulling at us in our weakest moments. The more success that comes our way, the more difficult it can be to combat pride and arrogance. In truth, God has used individuals throughout history to enact some dramatic changes in the world. We've already looked at some of them. However, those same individuals had their own difficulties. We are so uncomfortable with the thought of dependency on a single leader because we all know from history how many times it has ended badly.

For those of us who give any weight to godly ambition and a drive within us that disdains the status quo and yearns to push forward the things of God, we are left with the potential of pride becoming part of the mix. Especially since any level of success, will foster naturally an environment for pride. Because many true leaders burn for a cause, failure is rarely an attractive option on the road to that success.

Some of you will bristle at the notion of success, especially in the church world, but I think most of us fool ourselves here. It's why we go to the big conferences and follow the big churches and read the best books and blogs on church growth. There is, I know, an honorable part of all of us that encourages us to learn and grow so we can become the most effective in the places that we lead. But deep down, really deep down, our yearning for success is a little more defined than just being faithful.

There is in the heart of most leaders, a subtle yearning for recognition, especially for the tireless work and efforts we exact. And the fear of failure can have a debilitating effect on our value and self-worth. Not only do we see it as a personal and organizational failure, but we also see it as failing God.

Failure does, though, have a very important role to play in the life cycle of a leader. It's something we will look at in the pages ahead, but for now, I want to keep pushing the dangers that pride and arrogance invite, especially in relation to infidelity. So how do we develop ourselves as the kind of leaders we need to be, while at the same time being sold out for the mission, without allowing the entire enterprise to become a personal venue for self-aggrandizement? Especially in the world of social media?

There was a time that you were able to promote a book based on the premise of an idea. Now, however, one of the key components that becomes part of assessing whether a publisher will take a risk on your work is the size of your platform. In other words, the larger the platform the greater the likelihood they will look seriously at the investment. So, just to get published means lots of up front self-promotion. Obviously there are good and bad elements of this, but it does push you into a state of self-promotion and advertising.

I've Been Tempted To …

I know I've focused on the topic of pride and arrogance for a number of chapters now, but I think we've downplayed the static it creates in the background. Ask yourself this one question: Why does the Bible continually talk about loving others, serving with humility, having a life of integrity, learning to forgive, and keeping away from things that are immoral, unethical, and ungodly, if they were easy and natural parts of our make-up? There is a constant message to focus on others, to direct your thoughts and actions on others, otherwise there is looming danger for someone who is more concerned about themselves. Even a casual observer of biblical truth recognizes this.

Remember the story of the Trojan Horse at the beginning of the book? For all the focus placed upon that wooden horse it is by no means the core reason the Greeks were able to win the war. The horse, and the scheme that went with it targeted the pride of the Trojans. The very quality that ignited in their warriors a fierce resolve to defend their city, their people, their way of life, their honor, and anything else their pride elevated, was the one characteristic, when pacified, that caused them to drop their guard. Even when others tried to warn the leaders.

It bears repeating that the ploy of the Trojan Horse was to elevate the pride of the Trojans. The message it sent was, "You're the better warriors," "You've beaten us finally," "You've won," "We give up and are leaving!" "The gods have favored you!" Ask yourself if you could have resisted the tendency of pride clouding your judgement in such a moment of celebration and victory?

Pride can leave us open to deception. It is one of the fastest means of self-sabotage. We can be deceived and fall for temptation, and we can be deceived and fall for idolatry. Both are versions of infidelity. On the personal level, I want to expand the notion of infidelity beyond the idea of a spouse who cheats on their partner. Infidelity is much more. It is any institution or organization, personal or public, that you have made a commitment to, where you as a leader are unfaithful to its vows, laws, or stated beliefs.

Notice that the commitment is not defined by you. For instance, in marriage there are vows. They state the rules of commitment: For better for worse, for richer for poorer, sickness and in health, and so forth. These are what you commit to. You breach those vows whenever your conduct over time goes against what you've vowed to uphold. Harsh, yes, but that is exactly what vows are to protect and prepare us for.

Take someone who leads a company, whose standards of ethics are well stated as well as the financial policies of the organization. Is it not infidelity for that leader, who is well aware of the rules, if he is caught embezzling the company's money?

For most of us, infidelity is often relegated to personal indiscretions of adultery. We are expanding the notion of infidelity to include anything where we are found cheating. As a leader, those whom you lead, or have authority over, expect you to abide by a certain code of ethics and standards. And even though politicians, business leaders, and leaders of all sectors have failed the fidelity test in the past, we continue to be upset because we continue to expect better. So, as a leader, why not consider being a part of the solution instead of helping to perpetuate the problem?

Infidelity here is not limited to sexual indiscretions, as we've said, but to any behaviour that betrays the norm, displaces trust, or perverts the sanctity of an organization's ethics or values. In the Bible, the notion of adultery wasn't simply the act of sex outside of marriage; it also denotes falling for the extravagances of our culture without restraint, as well as worshipping anything other than God.[1] Pride feeds the potential of falling for temptation, which ultimately causes infidelity. Hence the continual warnings in the Bible about temptation and idolatry, and the ever present call to embrace humility.

Seeing Clearly

No one wants to be guilty of infidelity, whether personally or professionally. Yet, time and again, smart, talented, faithful people are falling prey to it. Let's start looking at some practical ways to help guard our hearts. I want to reiterate again that leadership is far too important a responsibility for us to take lightly. People are depending on strong leaders who have integrity and strength of character and God, especially, desires men and women who serve with faith and dignity.

As leaders who want to lead well, we are naturally going to bump up against pride. And when we do we need to be aware of the doors it will lead us through. We've seen how it affected the lives of David and Solomon, so let's list the possible ways it could affect you.

Pride makes temptation look less menacing

Temptation itself is not a sin, but falling for it is. There's not one of us who doesn't battle daily with temptation. It can provoke us to behave unethically, immorally, selfishly, and hastily. We can be tempted to deal with others in an unconcerned, unloving manner. As a leader, these temptations will affect your ability to lead others with integrity.

Here's why. Pride promotes a view of superiority over others, that we are better in some way, or we deserve more and are entitled to more. Because you feel that way, and if that feeling is left to solidify, you end up with a spirit of entitlement and an absence of accountability.

When we are then confronted with temptation, it becomes easier to yield to it because we feel we deserve it. We can rationalize very easily the reasons why it's okay to have the affair, take the bribe, or cheat on the balance sheet. Invariably, falling into the trap of temptation always sets in motion the collateral damage that inevitably comes with it, but is rarely considered in the midst of being tempted.

Which is why the Bible pushes so hard in the direction of serving others. Because whenever we allow pride to govern our leadership, we will invariably commit infidelity to the very people to who we are responsible. It becomes a vicious cycle that we've seen many times before.

There is something unnerving about temptation. The emotions that are heightened in the moment cause us to lose all objectivity because there is always more to the temptation than what we see in the moment. Each time we are tempted we are putting something in jeopardy-our marriage, our career, our reputation. Yet somehow we are willing to risk it all. The thoughts that predominate our thinking are, "I deserve this," "No one will ever know," "It's just this once," and so on.

This is why character always trumps talent. Talent alone lends itself to elevating pride, but character is not an isolation enterprise. Character is recognized by the world you engage in. And the development of character fosters a sense of serving others and taking them into consideration above yourself. This becomes a means of safe guarding the potential of committing infidelity against those you lead.

Pride devalues sin, but sin has consequences — even after forgiveness. As we saw with David and Solomon, these were the highest ranking men in the nation, but even they could not escape the consequences of their actions. And if the highest authorities of the land could not get away with their indiscretions, why do we believe we will get away with ours?

Pride makes idolatry more inviting

As grievous as committing infidelity against one another is the infidelity we commit against God. Any created thing in our lives that takes the place of God is an idol. Ask yourself these questions:

1. Is there something in my life that I can't live without, so much so that I would rather die than lose it?
2. Will my life lose all purpose, direction, and meaning if I lose it?
3. Does it compete with God and win?
4. Does it consume my thinking?
5. Have I taken a good thing and made it into an "ultimate thing?"

If you've answered yes to any of those questions you are likely struggling with an idol. Infidelity against God is not something I believe we should take lightly. It is so easy to look at the world of non-believers and see the idols they have in their lives.

It only stands to reason that we need to replace emptiness in our lives with something. We may never recognize the emptiness, but we all sense a need for something. So it shouldn't surprise us whenever we tend to elevate work, money, the environment, or family, to places of paramount importance. Because we ultimately become whatever we worship.

I will never forget early on in my pastoral career when I was in the midst of a message on idolatry. I was relating the idols of today's culture when I mentioned children and pets as two of the worst. Oops. You could have heard a pin drop. I could literally feel the room freeze up. I probably should have eased into that hot button topic before blurting it out.

To this day I am quite amazed at what will upset people in church.

What I've found is that, more often than not, the idols of our culture will get me more emails and harsh comments if I say anything against them. It is far easier to speak against sin and to promote needing a Saviour and getting your life right than to say that you've committed adultery against God because you've idolized your kids, your job, your money, your family, your smart phone, your education, your house, your car, the environment, and the list goes on.

Let's be clear, there are many wonderful and good things that we have in this world. God has given so much to enjoy and celebrate. But when those good things, become ultimate things, we are in trouble. Pride in the spiritual world is no less a problem. So much of what we do can easily become more important than God, and suddenly our *ministries* become our source of identity, instead of God. I like how Tim Keller frames this topic when speaking on MSNBC's Morning Joe show:

> When you make your work your identity ... if you're successful it destroys you because it goes to your head. If you're not successful it destroys you because it goes to your heart—it destroys your self-worth. [Faith in Christ] gives you an identity that's not in work or accomplishment, and that gives you insulation against the weather changes. If you're successful, you stay humble. If you're not successful, you have some ballast .... Work is a great thing when it is a servant instead of a lord.[2]

It's true that many church leaders begin as faithful to Christ's call on their lives. But it is easy to fall prey to making the work become our identity, particularly if it is in any way successful. We can even rationalize the growth and success as God's blessing while deep inside, if God were to remove it, we would be demoralized.

In *Liberating Ministry from the Success Syndrome*, the case is stated wonderfully by Kent Hughes:

> Years earlier when I began the ministry the motivation was simply to serve Christ. That was all…All I wanted was the approval of God. But imperceptibly my high Christian idealism had shifted from serving to receiving, from giving to getting. I realized that what I really wanted was a growing church and "success" more than the smile of God…I realized that I had been subtly seduced by the secular thinking that places a number on everything. Instead of evaluating myself and my ministry from God's point of view, I was using the world's standard of qualitative analysis.[3]

We recognize in this passage what's being alluded to, the deceptive allure of pride that comes with the desire to succeed in most leaders. It's a desire that begins as honorable, but can migrate very easily into infidelity towards God and his kingdom work.

David and Solomon's stories serve as a cautionary tales, demonstrating that God takes spiritual infidelity seriously. I also believe this to be one of the reasons the early church was so effective. Most people point to the Spirit of God and to the miracles, but frankly, these are still operational today. The Spirit of God hasn't left and the potential of miracles is still there if God so chooses, but the early churches ability to identify and separate themselves from the idols of their day is a key element we've ignored in their effectiveness.[4] We, on the other hand, are continually being accused of looking just like the culture we're a part of.

Pride elevates our position to God-like status

Part of our dilemma when it comes to idols is the question, "Does God truly satisfy every need I have?" This is a core question, and one that is at the heart of temptation and idolatry. I think this is one of the key reasons we are seeing such a decline in belief today. There was a time when we believed we were answerable to God, now the tables are turned and many people act as if God is answerable to us. Human pride tempts us to treat our relationship with God with indifference or disrespect.

The burden of proof rests with God now. He must answer for why there is evil or why the world is as it is. In fact, much of the prevailing attitude is that God has made a mess of things and the human race will have to put it right. We have brought our human wisdom to bear on the necessity for God, because for most, they have everything they need to live a fulfilling life without him.

Those of us in the church world can fall into the same type of trap. Ministry is hard, not just because it deals with people, but also because of the difficulty it places on family life. I was in management positions and self-employed before going into ministry, but I have never been probed privately the way I have been in the church.

I've intentionally used the term probed because it has been so intrusive at times that I've felt like those people who've been abducted by aliens and tell stories of the experiments that were performed on them. Never in my years of employment outside the church was I ever scrutinized to the degree I have been in church. As difficult as it has been for me, it has been especially hard on my family. Not necessarily saying the degree of scrutiny is wrong, I'm aware of what's at stake, but the lack of sensitivity has caused me pause.

Because ministry can be so difficult, the victories, no matter how modest, can become the most gratifying part of what we do. But it can detract from finding our meaning and purpose in Christ alone. Because what I find is that the more driven we are as a leader, the greater the danger of becoming prideful. And sometimes we've quenched and warned so much against a spirit of wanting to succeed for God that we've actually tamed the environment to mediocrity.

Trust is lost with infidelity

It really goes without saying that whenever we commit an act of infidelity we have lost the trust of those we've hurt. But for leaders, trust foundational. When we commit infidelity we are stating that we do not have the character or competence to perform with integrity the duties entrusted to us.

There are many resources that you can turn to for dealing with this topic, but for our purposes I want to deal with one element of it. A church leader, who falls for temptation, has already decided that God could not be trusted to take care of them. The degree in which we believe God is the degree in which we will be able to stave off temptation.

Temptation causes us to ask whether or not God's promises can be trusted. Can I believe what he says, and do I have the confidence in him to resist the temptation and not fall? The issue of trust is often treated as a matter after the fact, but for a church leader first and foremost is their faith and trust in God. These are issues to resolve prior to falling into temptation, otherwise, when it comes, there will be little to help you resist. You see, no one will really trust a church leader, until they've demonstrated their ultimate trust in God first.

Taking Control

It would be helpful at this juncture to differentiate between power and authority. We can sometimes find ourselves having difficulty distinguishing between the two. James Hunter in *The World's Most Powerful Leadership Principle*, defines them this way:

Power is the ability to force or coerce others to do your will, even if they would choose not to, because of your position or might.

141

Authority is the skill of getting others willingly to do your will because of your personal influence.[5]

Power and authority are often interrelated but to define them in this way dramatically shifts the focus. As Hunter points out, power can be bought and sold, given and taken away.[6] It can reside with someone simply because they feel more privileged due to status or position.

I came across a study that links power with infidelity. Though it specifically deals with sexual infidelity, I would argue that the same mechanics apply to infidelity of any kind. Because power breeds pride which this article terms as confidence.

> Data from a large survey of 1,561 professionals were used to examine the relationship between power and infidelity and the process underlying this relationship. Results showed that elevated power is positively associated with infidelity because power increases confidence in the ability to attract partners. This association was found for both actual infidelity and intentions to engage in infidelity in the future. Gender did not moderate these results: The relationship between power and infidelity was the same for women as for men, and for the same reason. These findings suggest that the common assumption (and often-found effect) that women are less likely than men to engage in infidelity is, at least partially, a reflection of traditional gender-based differences in power that exist in society.[7]

There are instances where power works. You can even likely get away with exercising it for a season, but its downside is that it eventually damages relationships. Authority on the other hand is quite different. It can't be bought or sold, given or taken away. Authority is about you as a person. It's about your character.[8] In some of the literature they use the term influence in much the same manner but the understanding is the same. The best leaders, are the ones who invest in their character, because they are the ones who will best be able to resist the lure of pride, thus guarding their hearts from temptation and idolatry.

We discussed the hazards of committing infidelity, both personally to the people around you and spiritually to the God we serve, and also the mechanisms that prompt us to succumb to temptation and idolatry. Still, many leaders who are dynamic and driven will struggle with a tendency towards pride. But what we learned a couple of chapters back is that humility provides the best antidote to pride, arrogance, and hubris.

I once heard the adage "small hinges swing big doors" though I can't recall where. The phrase has stuck with me. I think this applies so well to the call for humility in a leader's life. Whenever we adopt a posture of humility, it has the potential to swing large doors open. It can create an atmosphere that isn't governed by fear, but by honesty and teamwork. It can repair a long standing conflict or reinstate a group's trust and faith.

So much can transpire when we commit to a life of humility that the potential it can have on your leadership can only be fully measured over time. In *Rescuing Ambition*, Dave Harvey gives a wonderful insight on the place of humility against ambition. As we stated above, dynamic leaders have great ambition, but can often get in trouble if pride overtakes a humility before God. Harvey believes that ambition and humility need to be rescued from our current understanding. I couldn't agree more.

Ambition must also be rescued from a wrong understanding of humility. That may sound crazy, but I'm serious. I think this issue quenches a lot of evangelical fire. Humility, rightly understood shouldn't be a fabric softener on our aspirations. When we become too humble to act, we've ceased being biblically humble. True humility doesn't kill our dreams; it provides a guardrail for them, ensuring that they remain on God's road and move in the direction of his glory.[9]

Infidelity can potentially become a Trojan Horse, and anytime you allow infidelity to diminish your capacity to lead from your strengths, it undermines your ability to lead well, or to lead at all.

CHAPTER 10

Insert Foot ...

When Simon Peter realized what had happened, he fell to his knees before Jesus and said, "Oh, Lord, please leave me--I'm too much of a sinner to be around you." (Luke 5:8)

We have spent the last number of chapters evaluating the lives of Abraham, Moses, David, and Solomon, real people whom God used to accomplish amazing things. Each had their failings, which we've highlighted in detail, but few have the kind of reputation for epic failure like Peter.

As one of Jesus' twelve disciples he was part of his inner circle. A man who became a champion of the early church and who tradition says was crucified upside down. His story is not an easy one to critique, mostly due to the kind of individual he was.

For all his good intentions, there are moments when he is either doing, or saying the wrong things. Peter seems to represent the best and the worst in all of us. We can relate easily to his frailties, be shocked the next minute at his courage, be inspired by his proclamations, and be dumbfounded the next by his failures.

In fact I have to admit that for the most part, Peter, of all the characters in the Bible, confounds me the most. He seems difficult to gauge and utterly compulsive. He rides his emotions openly and at times would anger Jesus with ridiculous statements. I've joked many times that Peter was often putting the proverbial sandal in his mouth! Then, mere moments later, he is making a revelation that cements his place in biblical history.

Passionate, yet brash, impulsive, yet pensive, this is the same man who ended up denying Jesus three times, a detail that has become integral to the crucifixion story. Here is this man Peter, the leader of Jesus' band of twelve men, part of his inner circle, doing the unthinkable.

As I've read the various accounts of Peter's life in a number of commentaries and scholarly works, I'm intrigued at the predominance of writers who virtually ignore the inconsistencies of this man. Is it just me? They may take a poke at him here and there but for the most part few like to talk about the extent of his ups and downs.

For me, Peter is a classic example why I admire Jesus so much. Peter would have driven me crazy and I would likely have been able to tolerate him in short spurts. But Jesus takes this impulsive and sometimes reckless human and moulds him into one of the most focused, humble, yet dynamic purveyors of the Christian message. To accomplish it even after Peter's betrayal is amazing to comprehend.

A person who would have exasperated my tolerance for drama is one of the most revealing character studies for leadership. Primarily due to the degree his life swings from failure one moment, then to radical disciple who is changing the world the next.

Working with What You Have

With respect to the Gospels, they reveal the centrality of Peter in many key situations. For a long time I wondered why Peter was given so much airtime. His sometimes undisciplined actions weren't exactly complimentary, nor was some of what he said. For Jesus, some of his harshest words were specifically aimed at Peter.

Nonetheless, as a leader, Peter should encourage you. His gradual transformation was not smooth or without deep pain, but what came out the other side is worth noting. There are volumes that focus on Peter's ultimate contribution to the history of the church, but for our purposes I want to centre on the development of his leadership. Which means digging deeper into the biblical portrayal of his human side.

Peter's humanity is prominently displayed. Again, I'm well aware that God is the ultimate focus of the biblical text, but some of the greatest lessons are learned through the way he uses people that are committed to him. No matter how fractured their lives seem. Which is why Peter's life as a leader is so valuable to investigate.

Part of the difficulty with Peter is what do you focus on? Guilt, shame, aggressiveness, compulsion, lack of discipline, good intentions? The potential sweep of this man's emotional catalog is something to behold. But beyond the peaks and valleys, Jesus saw something in him that eventually was shaped and honed, propelling him to prominence not only as a key disciple, but as the rock of the early church.

In the years that I've studied Peter his tendency for impulsiveness and acting without forethought have grown more evident. He was a man of the moment if there ever was one and whatever his gut told him, he acted on it right away. When I looked up impulsive in a thesaurus it gave me these words: impetuous, spontaneous, hasty, passionate, emotional, uninhibited; rash, reckless, careless, imprudent, foolhardy, unwise, madcap.[1]

I couldn't help but laugh when I read the entry. All those describe the portrait of Peter we have in Scripture. They all encompass the life of Peter's in one graphic mosaic.

For the sake of simplicity then, I've taken the various accounts of Peter and grouped them into three major categories. In each there is an "extreme" element. When Peter succeeded it was spectacular; when he failed it was equally spectacular. There seems to be no middle ground for this disciple. As we go through the categories I'm assuming that you are familiar with the stories and will give references, but I'll try to make each summary understandable on its own.

Extreme Stories

As part of the Gospel narratives we get these incredible narratives that draw us into the suspense of the moment. In many cases Peter is part of it. One such example is found in Matthew 14:22-32, a great story that incorporates together the tensions between faith, risk, doubt, and fear. The disciples are in a boat with a storm raging in the middle of the night. They suddenly see walking on water what they think at first is a ghost. Jesus admonishes the guys to "not fear" and to "take courage because Jesus is with them!"

I'm not sure what Peter was thinking, but of the twelve, Peter is the one who straightaway sees what Jesus is doing and wants part of the action too. Upon Jesus' invitation, Peter gets out of the boat and starts walking on water. He gets so far until he suddenly comes to his senses and realizes that the storm is still in full throttle. When that awareness strikes him he begins to sink and Jesus has to save him. With that, Jesus rebukes Peter for doubting and lacking faith.

I personally can't get over Peter's initial act of getting out of the boat. It's indicative of the type of impulsiveness that pulls him without restraint into situations. It's not until he has walked on the water for a bit that he's jolted by the reality of what he's doing. We often look at Jesus' words to Peter about lacking faith as a dismissal of Peter's actions. I somehow think for Jesus it was an optimal teaching moment to remind Peter about his need to focus.

There is a verse as part of the story that keeps me shaking my head every time I read it:

Then Peter called to him, "Lord, if it's really you, tell me to come to you, walking on the water." (Matthew 14:28)

Now I love Peter, but let me ask you something. Peter calls out and says, "Jesus, if it's you." As proof, Peter thinks the best test is to walk on water? Timeout! I don't know about you but I can think of easier tests to find out whether it was Jesus or not? Personally I would have asked trick questions like, "What did we have for dinner?" "Name the other guys in the boat," or "What's my mother's name?" Not sure my first thought would have been taking a walk on the water in the midst of a storm.

Pretty impulsive if you ask me. Notice, too, that Jesus doesn't say to Peter, "Hang on a minute while I make the sea a little less choppy for you!" There are few moments in the Bible that illustrate the tension between faith, fear, and risk better than Peter's walk on water. In this one story, the lessons that are gleaned because of Peter's impulsiveness are hard to match.

Let us not forget something else. Peter can always say he's walked on water. That's something he has over the other eleven guys in the boat. It's an experience that no one can ever take away from him, even if you want to be a pessimist and see it ending as an ultimate failure. For my money, Peter learned a lesson that helped shape his leadership to come, something missed by the others.

Extreme Statements

We get to hear quite a bit from Peter. Sometimes it's good, other times not so much. But as with all things Peter, when it is good, it's revelatory, and when it's not, well you get the picture. I've often wondered about the reason for Peter's profile as a spokesman. One reason I think is due to his impulsiveness. While the others are weighing whether they should speak, Peter's already blurted out what the group is likely thinking. He seems to be the one that appears to have the least amount of problem getting his tongue to work before his brain. To his credit, that same eagerness to blurt out his first impulse, also lands him the legacy of some of the most profound statements from a disciple.

One of Peter's stellar moments comes in Matthew 16:13-20. The gang has just ventured into Caesarea Philippi, a hot bed of Roman paganism and shrines. The evidence would have been hard to miss, but Jesus chooses this particular backdrop to ask his disciples essentially what the rumours are about him?

After the disciples have listed some possibilities, Jesus asks more directly, "But who do *you* say I am?" It's at that prompting that Peter speaks:

Simon Peter answered, "You are the Messiah, the Son of the living God." (Matthew 16:16)

That is a spiritual home-run for Peter. This is the ultimate test that Jesus presents and Peter hits it out of the park. In fact, Jesus is so pleased with what he hears, look at his response.

Jesus replied, "You are blessed, Simon son of John, because my Father in heaven has revealed this to you. You did not learn this from any human being. Now I say to you that you are Peter (which means 'rock'), and upon this rock I will build my church, and all the powers of hell will not conquer it. And I will give you the keys of the Kingdom of Heaven. Whatever you forbid on earth will be forbidden in heaven, and whatever you permit on earth will be permitted in heaven." Then he sternly warned the disciples not to tell anyone that he was the Messiah. (Matthew 16:17-20)

Now, let me repeat this again. There are volumes of great scholarly works that deal with all the theological and exegetical nuances of the text. My focus is somewhat different, because what has always amazed me is looking at the text from the perspective of Peter himself. What would he have heard in all this?

First of all, as much as many want to deny it, Peter is marked here for something significant. Not only had God given Peter a direct revelation, but there was also a significant role for Peter to play in the future. He may not have understood the entire depth and breadth of what that would entail, but I can't imagine that Peter would not have been pumped! The disciples as a whole would have seen that moment as a kind of watershed event.

Without getting into all the details of the text I believe the overall message Peter would have heard is that, "I have a plan for you," "it's going to include something great," "so much so that it will rattle the very gates of hell," and "you are going to play a major role in making it happen." "It will have the power of God behind it and it's going to be awesome!"

That's what I believe would have echoed in the heart of Peter at that moment. But the caveat to the entire picture is making sure to remember that Jesus is the Messiah, the Son of God. Because without that critical piece, Peter's role would not be as potent.

Here is what else is daunting. Jesus spends considerable time with his disciples, explaining as much as he can so they will comprehend the events that are about to unfold. For the most part, they never truly "got it" until the resurrection and the initiation of the church. I've often wondered how many times over the course of his time with Jesus did Peter look back at this moment wondering when it would all come together?

Which is why what follows in the Matthew text is so fascinating. Remember we said that Peter has moments of brilliance, then says something which leaves you wondering if it's the same guy? Following is another story in Matthew 16:22-23. The passage opens with Jesus beginning to teach his disciples what will transpire concerning him. That he will experience terrible suffering, be handed over to be crucified, and then be raised again on the third day. Frankly, from the view of the disciples, that would have been a lot to handle. And in true form, Peter enters the fray.

> But Peter took him aside and began to reprimand him for saying such things. "Heaven forbid, Lord," he said. "This will never happen to you!" 23 Jesus turned to Peter and said, "Get away from me, Satan! You are a dangerous trap to me. You are seeing things merely from a human point of view, not from God's." (Matthew 16:22-23)

What I think is clear here is the fact that Peter's expectations of what it means for Jesus to be the Messiah don't square with what Jesus is saying. But as praiseworthy as Jesus is in the first story, he is just as forceful against Peter in the second. What was revealed by God in the earlier text allows Peter to hear the full rendering of what the future holds for God's plan.

Here, because it's driven by human perception, Jesus hurls the title of Satan at him. I don't know about you but I've had a lot of names thrown at me, done a lot of stupid things, and made a lot of people angry. Can't say I've ever been called Satan, though!

I don't want to discount the theological import of these stories, but I think something else is going on too. Jesus' high language in the first text, and his harsh accusations in the next are exactly what an impulsive guy like Peter needs to hear. He has to learn to be jolted out of his impulse to react and to think logically. True, he may not grasp the full breadth of each passage, but Jesus needs to stress to him the importance on relying on the Godly things, and being suspect of those impulses that are humanly driven.

That is why I have so much respect for Jesus. He is no doubt a master teacher, but how he shapes the life of Peter continues to be a wonder throughout the Bible's pages. It is this incident that prompts Jesus to recite some of the best known words concerning what it will take to follow him.

> Then Jesus said to his disciples, "If any of you wants to be my follower, you must turn from your selfish ways, take up your cross, and follow me. If you try to hang on to your life, you will lose it. But if you give up your life for my sake, you will save it. And what do you benefit if you gain the whole world but lose your own soul? Is anything worth more than your soul? (Matthew 16:24-26)

Extreme Shortcomings

Peter does end up in many cases being the foil to Jesus. There are times of great and profound teaching from Jesus that are initiated by something Peter said or did. Case in point is John 13, the well known account of Jesus washing the disciples feet.

I have told my students for years that if you want to learn about leadership in the church don't go first to 1 and 2 Timothy or Titus. There are two passages they need to be filtered through. The first is Deuteronomy 17:14-20, a passage where Moses outlines the stipulations for a king. The second is the foot washing passage in John 13. They form the foundational structure for every other leadership passage in the Bible, and we would do well to review them from time to time.

The contrasts in John 13 are hard to ignore. John begins the passage by reminding his readers of Jesus' deity, that the Father had given authority over everything into his hands. Remember I've said that every detail counts. John is reminding us that Jesus is God incarnate and the power that resides with God resides with Jesus as well.

That little detail is not inconsequential, because what's about to happen is going to strike a dramatic contrast that Peter is not going to be able to bear. Jesus removes his robe and wraps a towel around himself. What Jesus began to do was reserved for slaves, it was menial work. And what is more striking to me is Jesus not only performs the menial task but dresses down for it as well. What began as a reminder of Jesus' ultimate power has now turned into a picture of humble service. The contrast could not have been more stunning. If a stranger had of walked in the room, he would naturally assume that Jesus was the servant of this group of men, not their leader, let alone God incarnate.

But as Jesus approaches Peter he finds him less than receptive.

"No," Peter protested, "you will never ever wash my feet!" Jesus replied, "Unless I wash you, you won't belong to me." Simon Peter exclaimed, "Then wash my hands and head as well, Lord, not just my feet!" (John 13:8-9)

The moment that Jesus has taken to wash the disciples feet is thought by some scholars to transpire right at the time of ceremonial cleansing during the Passover meal. If so, Peter should recognize the solemnity of the moment. Regardless, I'v always been struck by Peter's overstatement in verse 9.

Having first objected to Jesus washing his feet, and Jesus rebuking him for not allowing it, he then says what must be one of the dumbest things possible. I personally believe this is a classic reaction of an impulsive man who's not quite grasping the full import of the moment.

But again, to Jesus' credit, he uses the awkward moment from Peter to shape his understanding about what all this means.

Jesus replied, "A person who has bathed all over does not need to wash, except for the feet, to be entirely clean. And you disciples are clean, but not all of you." For Jesus knew who would betray him. That is what he meant when he said, "Not all of you are clean." After washing their feet, he put on his robe again and sat down and asked, "Do you understand what I was doing?

> You call me 'Teacher' and 'Lord,' and you are right, because that's what I am. And since I, your Lord and Teacher, have washed your feet, you ought to wash each other's feet. I have given you an example to follow. Do as I have done to you. (John 13:10-15)

Here's what I'm going to propose. The embarrassing comment from Peter becomes a launch point for Jesus to teach a deeper truth. What Peter said was purely impulsive, but Jesus was able to re-direct it in a way that I believe would have stuck with Peter more. One of the reasons I feel this way is from my readings of 1 Peter. Whenever he presents the believer's responsibility to serve others, it is peppered with the humility that would have been learned from an experience such as this.

I don't believe that the lessons that Jesus taught the disciples, and Peter especially, were totally lost on them. The resurrection brought them fully to light. In 1 Peter 5 especially, we read the writings of an elder who calls others to shepherd God's flock in the type of humble service demonstrated in John 13.

Of the patterns in Peter's life where impulsiveness brought

him angst, none comes back to haunt him more than this exchange between himself and Jesus:

"Simon, Simon, Satan has asked to sift each of you like wheat. But I have pleaded in prayer for you, Simon, that your faith should not fail. So when you have repented and turned to me again, strengthen your brothers." (Luke 22:31-32)

Just prior to this the disciples had been arguing about who would be the greatest among them. I have to think that there was a spirit of competition with these guys. But as part of Jesus' response to them about being invited to dine with him in his kingdom he stops and centres out Peter. The challenge to Peter is great. It essentially says, "Peter, you are a target, Satan has you in his sights, you will go through extreme testing, but you will overcome."

At this juncture I likely would have asked some questions: "What do you mean Satan wants me?" "Why would you think my faith would fail?" "And what's this about repenting?" But no questions are asked, no probing as to the why of Jesus' plea, just this bold proclamation.

Peter said, "Lord, I am ready to go to prison with you, and even to die with you." (Luke 22:33)

Braver words have rarely been spoken, but Jesus knows better.

But Jesus said, "Peter, let me tell you something. Before the rooster crows tomorrow morning, you will deny three times that you even know me." (Luke 22:34)

What happens after these statements is well documented. In one of the most difficult reversals in history the very person who claimed his allegiance the boldest is also the one to deny him the loudest. Three times in fact. It is one of the more epic failures in the Biblical record.

Extreme Similarities

What I want to stress at this point is the effects that failure had on Peter. We will not see its full ramifications until some time from now, and a key meeting must happen first in order for the full breadth of his guilt to be assuaged.

Before we go there I want to bring to your attention an important commonality in the writings about the disciples. Peter's journey with Jesus matches another's in somewhat of a disturbing parallel. Peter is the leader of the disciples, the proverbial good guy, one with whom we all identify. If you were to ask which disciple was on the opposite end of the spectrum the obvious answer is Judas, a man whose name has become synonymous with betrayal.

But of the twelves disciples, the life of Peter matches most closely with that of Judas.

- Both were disciples of Jesus (Matt 4:18-19; Mark 3:16-19; Luke 6:13-16)

- Both betrayed Jesus (Matthew 26:14-16; 33-35; 47-49; 73-74; John 6:71; 13:2)

- Both felt remorse for what they had done (Matt 27:3; Luke 22:60-62)

Though some would see Peter's betrayal as lesser than that of Judas's, its betrayal nonetheless. Despite their similarities, both ended very differently. Judas hanged himself (Matthew 27:5; Acts 1:18-19), but Peter carried on (John 21; Acts 2:14; 3:6; 4:8; Gal 2:7-9)

Peter's response in the end was very different. Although he was deeply wounded by what he had done, he still carried on — he still persevered. Judas on the other hand, though he felt remorse, ended up hanging himself. Even though he was deeply hurt by what he had done, Peter distinguishes himself from Judas. We are told that Judas was prompted by the Devil and became an instrument of God's plan (John 13:2). However, the Book of Matthew does present him as remorseful for betraying Jesus, whom he recognizes is an innocent man (Matt 27:4). I would like to believe that had Judas not hanged himself, he would have had a chance at redemption. But that opportunity never came because he took the matter into his own hands.

At the beginning of John 21, we find Peter fishing again on the Sea of Galilee. It's a familiar scene, not unlike an earlier one in Matthew 4:18, when Jesus called out to two brothers fishing on the same sea, Peter and Andrew, and invited them to become fishers of people. Jesus is about to bring the invitation home to Peter in a way he would never have imagined.

Recall

The transformation of Peter is a sight to behold. And the passage that brings the entire experience of Peter to its zenith is found in John 21. From here, the Peter we witness is different. By the time we've arrived in the Book of Acts, the lessons that have been poured into him and the experiences that went along with them have sunk deep and stuck. But before any of that could happen, Jesus had one last thing to do.

Jesus shows up on the shore again as the disciples are fishing. The resurrected Jesus, after having breakfast with his disciples, takes a moment to talk with Peter. The exchange is beautiful for it's absence of drama. Not once does Jesus hurl accusatory comments in Peter's direction, or even say to him, "What were you thinking?"

Instead, with incredible insight, Jesus drills at the very source of guilt that would have been swirling in the background of Peter's mind, a guilt compounded three times to represent the number of denials from Peter. Jesus with intent, asks Peter three times, "Do you love me?"

With each affirmative response from Peter, Jesus presents the cause and effect. If you do, "Then feed my lambs," "Feed my sheep". Those three repeated questions rest at the heart of what motivated and focused the heart of Peter, which was the love he proclaimed for Jesus. Not once, but three times, to directly counter the number of denials that needed to flush Peter's guilt. Jesus knew enough that if the question was posed only once, in Peter's mind, he would still need forgiveness for another two.

This is a type of recall for Peter. The same as a car manufacturer that has to correct a flaw. Once repaired, the vehicle is safe and road-worthy again. For Peter, the posture of shepherding the people of God fits. Even though he has experienced many hard knocks to get there. From the opening pages of the Book of Acts he plays a prominent role, and even conducts the first sermon in the newly formed New Testament church in Acts 2.

Peter's restoration in John 21 is full and complete. Three times Peter denies Jesus, three times Peter confirms his love for Jesus, and three times Jesus gives him the responsibility to care for the people, a lesson he learned well when you read 1 and 2 Peter.

The Power of Failure

We have observed the impulsiveness of Peter who had a tendency to commit too quickly. He's assertive, outspoken, and ambitious, to be sure. What Peter also carries is a charismatic personality. At times it serves him well, but Peter has been inconsistent and unreliable-two traits not necessarily good for a leader. His impulsiveness pulls him in whatever direction his feelings and emotions take him.

His strength as a leader is undeniable, but his maturity is questionable. This is the polarity that Jesus recognizes. The most zealous individual, carefully tutored and instructed, can become the most focused flame. But before Peter gets there, much has to happen to shake him from the impulse to react. In many ways his spirit needed to be broken, and then re-shaped without diminishing the fire that burned within. That would have been the real task that Jesus was confronted with. To make this wild and unpredictable fisherman, with all the potential energy he could exert, into a focused and committed leader.

Impulsiveness doesn't lend itself well to commitment, something that Peter exhibited on a number of occasions. He would stand with conviction at the time, but be a disappointment when the moment came to back up his words. It was this unreliability that needed to be corrected before Peter could become the leader that Jesus saw in him.

As bold and impulsive as Peter was, when he became focused, he transformed into the apostle primarily responsible for evangelizing the Jews. Now think about that for a minute. That task could not have fallen to anyone who was shy, reserved, or soft spoken. More to the point, in this regard Peter became the major voice to the Jews following Jesus. Not an easy responsibility to bear.

This could only have been accomplished by someone who had experienced the dejection of having failed. We don't give failure the credit it deserves. Frankly, our greatest lessons aren't just taught when we fail, but they become indelibly imprinted upon our hearts.

Peter reminds us that regardless of what we have, when surrendered to God, it's all you need. The critics could have said that Peter had no business being in ministry. How many would have held up his betrayal of Jesus as a judgement for life? How many would have remembered his cavalier actions and relegated him to the status of unworthy. And yet, I believe that because he experienced such failure, he could speak with power and authority.

He doesn't appear to be wracked with guilt when we get into Acts, rather he is bent on purpose. When he pens his letters he writes to his audience on the need for holiness and self-control. When he speaks to the crowds he talks about salvation and hope. The confidence that he exudes is evident, so clearly in fact, that its original force is felt in his writings some two thousand years later.

The major reason is because of what Peter experienced-the restoring grace of God. He knew what it meant to begin fresh, to be given a real second chance, and to not have the sins of the past define you, but rather, only serve to remind you of how far God has taken you.

Peter, experienced forgiveness from unfaithfulness and betrayal. Jesus rebuilt him and restored him and made him new. With all things that we surrender to Jesus our failures are never fatal. We saw how Jesus took this reckless fisherman and made him not only a fisher of people, but a leader and shepherd as well.

He is an unlikely hero. But Jesus used him in great ways. He just needed time to shape him, that's all. In Acts 4:13, we read what is likely the best summary of those lives that Jesus touched. None more so than the man named Peter:

> The members of the council were amazed when they saw the boldness of Peter and John, for they could see that they were ordinary men with no special training in the Scriptures. They also recognized them as men who had been with Jesus. (Acts 4:13)

CHAPTER 11

The Trojan Horse of Impulsiveness

"Our most profitable lessons are learned from failure, not success." – *Frank Davidson*

"You get the best effort from others not by lighting a fire beneath them, but by building a fire within." – *Bob Nelson*

Ever done something you regret? Been there, done that. If you are like me the list is long and varied. Personally, some of the more poignant lessons in my life were those when I disappointed my dad. I can't say it happened often because my dad was a pretty gracious man, but there were times when I knew I had let him down.

One of the first times was when I was in my early teens. My dad wanted me to have my Canadian citizenship so he began the process for becoming a fully fledged Canadian. I was born in Athens and was a year old when my family migrated here.

During those turbulent teen years, though, I was having a rough time at school. The fact that I was a foreigner made me the focus of ridicule for some of my classmates. I can't repeat what creative skill they demonstrated with my last name. (Funny how that same inventiveness didn't relate to their schoolwork).

Nevertheless, the fact that I was feeling a bit sensitive about the whole foreigner label was something I never told my dad. The spotlight on bullying then was not anything like it is today. Both my brother and I were targets of some abusive behaviour, but when you're in your early teens its sometimes hard to know what's acceptable and what's not.

The day came when we arrived at the court to accept my citizenship. These many years later I am surprised at how few of the details I remember except for those I'm about to tell you. My dad was with me when my name got called. Imagine my horror when I realized that my dad had applied using my Greek name and not the anglicized version of it. Instead of Jon it was Iannis.

Well, in light of my heightened sensitivity I kind of lost it at that moment. I don't really know what happened other than to say I made my dad amply aware of my disapproval. Yes, I've always been kind of impulsive, and okay, maybe a bit of a hand-full, but even I didn't normally take to embarrassing my dad, especially in public. After a few awkward moments because of my tantrum, the judge, who witnessed the entire transaction, along with the others in the room, gave me a dressing down like I've never had since.

It wasn't a long speech, nor did it fully demoralize me. But it did put me in my place. It goes without saying that my citizenship papers reflected my father's wishes, and that was the end of the matter.

Something more happened. Every Canadian citizen at the time received a Bible. I took it and put it in my room when I got home. I forgot about it for some time. But one day when cleaning my room (yes, good Greek boys clean their room), I came across the Bible. It was the first time since the events of that day that I'd bothered to even open it. When I did I was surprised to find a little personal note from the judge written inside. A note that encouraged me to take the words of this book to heart, because that was the judge's prayer for me.

The Art of Reacting

That experience stayed with me. In many ways it was a precursor of what was to come. My family was Greek-Orthodox and went to church only on major holidays. It wasn't until years later that I would feel called to ministry. But it did open my eyes to the impulse I had for reacting, a problem I've wrestled with for years.

Peter, as we've seen, was impulsive. He would say or do the first thing that came into his head. And though he had strong leadership qualities, his knee jerk reactions would place him at odds with reality. Peter would say things and not back them up, the impulsiveness would damage his credibility.

In my mind this art of reacting is a leadership discipline that needs developing. There are so many contingencies that a leader is faced with today that our responses to their ebb and flow in our world will determine the effectiveness of what we do.

I've known a number of people like Peter. Lots of fire but little direction, lots of activity but little productivity. And not everyone has had the privilege of being directed and mentored by Jesus! Look what he accomplished with just twelve students.

But impulsiveness can easily lead to failures in judgement. Impulsiveness, when unbridled can leave a leader exposed to the danger of being driven purely by emotions. One of the great debates in the leadership world swirls around gut reactions. The tendency has been to adopt your inner instinct as a form of your leadership capability. In *Leadership Beyond Reason*, John Townsend posits the case for feelings and intuition playing a key role in any leaders development.

"Emotions not only can be helpful but also are a necessary part of successful leadership".[1]

For Townsend, this includes not only positive emotions, but negative ones as well. And if truth be known, I have greatest respect for leaders who best manage their emotions during crisis situations that would have caused most others to have a melt down. It is rarely helpful, regardless of the severity of the circumstances, to have a leader who's emotionally out of control.

In *Derailed*, Irwin demonstrates the contribution that a lack of self awareness and emotional intelligence has on the potential for failure, because most derailments are self-inflicted and precipitated by poor judgement.[2] Leaders who lack the discipline for self-management create a deficit in what they say and what they do.

Irwin further enlists Daniel Goleman's study of emotional intelligence, which, "generally comprises the capability to be self-aware, self-managing, interpersonally effective, stress tolerant, and optimistic."[3] From the research came these findings:

> ... EQ (Emotional Quotient or Intelligence), counts for 80-90 percent of the factors that distinguish average from outstanding leaders. His (Goleman), research indicates that the higher a leader rises in an organization, the less important technical skills become and the more important EQ becomes.[4]

In his book, *9 Things You Simply Must Do*, Henry Cloud writes on nine key principles he has observed in successful people. The first one (you guessed it), has to do with the internal life:

> ...The reality of the life we see and live on the outside is the one that emerges from the inside, from our hearts, minds, souls. It is our internal life that creates the external one. So, to find our lives we must find what lies below the surface of our skin. We must look at, listen to, discover, and be mindful of the internal life-such things as our talents, feelings, desires, and dreams.[5]

This is an important lesson to learn because the door to self-sabotage is opened through a leader's inability to regulate themselves, or at the very least be self-aware. Regardless of what sources you go to, whether the Bible or the Harvard Business Review, the importance of the internal life is the key difference in great leaders. And the ones who learn to regulate their strengths, temper their weaknesses, and gage their emotions without being overwhelmed by them, are the most effective leaders.

One trend I've noticed of late is the excessive rise of drama. I see it in my students, in my church, in my personal relationships…the malady appears everywhere. I'm not saying that everyone has it, but there is growing evidence of it. I don't know if it's harder to manage life and stress, or that people are just not taught how to cope, but it's a growing concern.

Excessive drama can become an opiate, a type of drug…even an idol. Like an addiction that demands its fix. I've been on many teams over the years, ministry, business, volunteer-and invariably the teams with the highest anxiety are the ones that have at least one high drama member. By high drama I mean someone who continually over-blows and exaggerates every situation or circumstance.

The older I get, the less tolerant I've become of drama. As a pastor, there's quite enough from normal life to keep things interesting. Yes, there are lots of things we could be wringing our hands over, but to continually be revving the engines on high over every single mishap is exhausting.

What I've found about those addicted to drama is that resolving their conflicts and keeping them satisfied is more difficult than others, resulting in more energy being diverted from real priorities and a heightened level of anxiety. After a while you end up with proximity poison from the over-exposure.

It's true, though, that the most difficult of all skills to master as a leader is the skill of leading yourself. It will be a challenge, but the rewards are well worth the effort. And again, there is too much at stake for the people and the organizations we lead to not take the investment in ourselves seriously.

One helpful tactic, especially in light of the topic currently discussed, is the *power of the pause*. It's the ability to take a step back before saying or doing anything and not allowing your first reaction to be the one that defines you.

I liken it to being in the woods and suddenly coming upon a rattle snake. What's your first impulse? To freeze. (At least it should be). You're suddenly afraid to make any sudden moves that will make your situation worse. In those frozen moments you're analyzing what to do. "Can I back up slowly?" "Do I just stay here till it moves away?" "Do I whack it with a stick?" Okay, maybe not the last one.

You get the idea. The prescience to pause, even briefly, may make all the difference in the world. We've all heard the advice to never send an email when angry. You can write it out, get it off your chest, but wait a day, reread it, and then see if you're comfortable sending it. The principle is the same. I know for me, the power of the pause has been a helpful way of limiting initial reactions.

Falling to Rise Again

Let's not discount what happens when we fail. I think failure is actually a vital component for growing leaders. And yet it's probably the one thing we fear the most. No one wants that on their conscience. Or their resume. I don't know when it happened, but the aversion to failure that I see around me makes me uneasy.

I've known work environments where the unwritten rules were, "Failure is not an option!" That phrase may be fine and inspiring when you're trying to save astronauts on a disabled craft, but it's not always good in the office. I can tell you from my own experience that this type of management created a level of anxiety that was extremely high. No one would attempt anything new for fear that it would fail and that every finger would point at them.

Every leader wants to be successful and to be known for excellence. However, it should not come at the expense of relationships, which unfortunately in many cases it does. If that's a consistent pattern for you, then it's time for a completely new philosophy. But that's a whole other book.

We've spent time looking at the importance of self-awareness in a leader. Yet, the best crash course in self-awareness often comes through failure. Few things cause us to reflect as long or as deeply as those times in life when we have felt ruined.

The questions that pervade your mind in those moments strike at the very heart of who you are. If you can't take into account what your part in the failure was, and instead resort to blaming everyone outside yourself, you will never learn to be self-aware. You will simply remain in your condition with little hope beyond your limited horizon.

One of the key insights from the characters of the Bible, regardless of who you're looking at, is anyone who accomplished anything for God was at one time a broken human being and a failure. Now, is this just what happens whenever you get religion? Or, could God know something about the human heart and the power of failure and brokenness?

Could it mean that for anyone to be used for any higher purpose we need to be purged of any baser ones? That may sound too altruistic for some, but the biblical record is consistent. And frankly from our own experiences, we know that when selfish ambition and motivation become rampant, the higher principles we strive to work for, really take a back seat.

Failure in many ways can be liberating. It can purge us of the very fear that has been lingering in our hearts all along. I'm not particularly fond of failing. Yet I have to admit, some of the more profound lessons in my life came from falling flat on my face. Every one of us, in order to be effective for God, will at some point experience our own "dark night of the soul."[6]

But most leaders don't handle failure well. And I don't think I'm being naive to believe that for the most part, we also struggle with guilt and forgiveness. I think it's a natural part of our human experience to feel the grief of failure. Even though, as Christian leaders, we have Christ as our hope and identity, God would not waste a valuable opportunity to teach us something through that grief.

After all, Jesus himself said that we too would suffer.[7] But the hurt that we feel from failure can leave deep scars on our hearts. Let me be clear. Failure can come in many forms and many guises. I'm not talking large catastrophic failures, but anything that gives you a sense of defeat. It could be relational, professional, organizational, staff, family…the list is endless.

Leaders, with a burden to make a difference in their world, have a tendency to feel the angst of failure more deeply than most. Nonetheless, while they may feel it more, they may tend to use it as a motivation to better themselves and learn the lessons from it, instead of becoming embittered.

You see, the tension for most dynamic leaders is found at both ends of the spectrum. On one hand, to be ambitious and driven to succeed at all costs will tend to move you into the potential danger of pride and arrogance. You will not appreciate those who think you are purely motivated by making a name for yourself. It becomes the ultimate question of whether or not you are building a monument to yourself or an altar to God.[8]

The other side of the tension is to inhibit your sense of ambition so you don't appear to be in it for your own glory. In these cases what ends up happening is, over time, your frustration grows because all you really end up doing is pacifying the people you lead, and never really accomplishing anything. This is called mediocrity, and frankly, we are already brimming with this malady in North America.

I've tried to put myself in Peter's sandals. I believe a majority of the pain that he would have felt was that he was damaged goods. He denied Christ while he was suffering. And yet, three days later Peter was peering into an empty tomb. He may have even felt that Jesus had wasted the three years he had invested in him, that there couldn't be any possible way that Christ would have any use for him now.

In John 21, Jesus recalls Peter to the role he's been mentoring him for, not allowing the failure to discard or make fruitless the years of training before hand. Now I'm not saying that every leader who fails deserves to be fully restored, but more often than not, a failure ends up defining us more than it should. Sometimes a failure is God's prescription for the moment, in order to teach you something for future effectiveness.

For all of my joking concerning Peter's propensity for drama, one thing about him is deadly serious. Peter is a man who takes his lumps and learns his lessons well. From John 21, the man we see after exhibits a focus that is unwavering as a key leader of the early church. Also, we do not see a hint of guilt or shame or bemoaning past failures. He presents a man whose forgiven, healed, given a second chance, and not wanting to waste a minute on feeling guilty. As demonstrated throughout Acts, and especially in 1 and 2 Peter, he is a man whose heart has been shaped for service and for God's glory.

Feeling like a failure is one thing, but staying there is another altogether. I'm not for a minute advocating that we don't take time to grieve whenever we've fallen. But to stay there and lack the resiliency to get back up is taking a good failure and wasting it! Even bouncing back for some of us is more out of duty than from being healed and re-energized.

Yes, it's something that will take time, and it will challenge our faith, but the process will be worth it. I think one of the most insulting things you can do to a leader who is feeling the guilt of failure is to throw a Bible verse at them and tell them to "get over it!" In fact, by doing that, you are actually compounding the guilt they are already feeling.

I remember some years back the funeral of a young man in our church who was killed in a car accident. It was tragic, because a number of youth were killed that day and I can still remember the incredible pain we all felt. The memorial service was packed. I decided not to go into the service, one, because the crowds were overwhelming, and two, my father had passed away that same week. I was numb to say the least.

Following the service, I heard that a group from the church down the road were there to pay their respects. What was disconcerting to me is that the pastor from that church berated his members for crying, because it was a betrayal of the Gospel which promises eternal life for believers. Wonder if he ever read John 11:35?

Failure can sometimes feel the same as when you've lost a loved one. The pain can be numbing, but to ignore it outright for the potential lessons that can be exacted from it, is to guarantee the failure has won.

Another reason why learning through failure is important, is that you are able to help others, because you've been there too. We all experience adversity of some kind. But when you are able to carry someone else through a difficult time it is one way of infusing hope into their lives.

I know that often we treat hope as a preferred future, but on a practical level, hope can also be a person. In another's eyes it can be you. There is great power in being able to identify with others, especially when they realize they are not the only ones who have experienced what they are going through.

At one of the churches in which I served, Darlene and I went through one of the darkest seasons of our lives. It was a very unhealthy situation. The transition that we had to make from that church was very painful, and it also had some peculiar circumstances attached to it. I never dreamed that it would ever be repeated. Oddly enough, a few years later, I met a pastor who was going through the same circumstances. I nearly fell over. I was able to walk him through how we managed the transition, and what he could expect down the road.

What Jesus did for Peter was give him hope. Peter needed that more than anything. He could have moved on, and that appeared to be the case. But he would have born the marks of his betrayal for the remainder of his years. And that's what leaders need as well-continual infusions of hope. Collins affirms this well when he writes:

> The signature of the truly great versus merely successful is not the absence of difficulty, but the ability to come back from setbacks, even cataclysmic catastrophes, stronger than before. Great nations can decline and recover. Great companies can fall and recover. And great individuals can fall and recover. As long as you never get entirely knocked out of the game, there remains always hope.[9]

For Collins the measure of hope is still available for the leader who is able to stay in the game. In his case, as he researches business environments he may be entirely right. From the standpoint of faith, failure is the end if we remove God from the equation.[10] No hope extends itself as the hope we are given in Christ. Peter came to see that clearly.

If you are a leader, and you are mentoring someone, I think a key element is to communicate, "I believe in you." Jesus did that for Peter. It's an important means of infusing hope. This simple posture transforms mentoring into a relationship for mutual benefit instead of an accountability relationship that essentially says, "I'm watching you, don't screw up!"

The P Word

Jesus gave something else to Peter that he desperately needed. Now before I tell you what that is I have to say this is the most painful section of the book to write. Not because this is going to aim for your jugular, but because I have to use a word I've come to despise. I couldn't even bring myself to put it in the title.

The word is ...*passion*. Now, it's not that this is a bad word in and of itself. But it's so overused, and abused. In fact, I believe that it's begun to venture into the realm of toxic. And just for clarity, I really did struggle even using the word for fear it has become toxic for you too.

From my observations, and perhaps it's just me, it seems everyone I talk to needs to express their passion to me (not romantically), and I've heard passion attached to things that have made me shake my head. I end up thinking, "Really, that's your passion? You are going to come to the end of your life and that's what you've dedicated your entire life too?"

I believe another word for passion could be burden, or even ambition. It was used by the previous generations of believers in the same way. As well, words like mission or vision, for some reflect the same idea as passion (although some would disagree and say passion includes much more).

Now, because I'm uncomfortable being fair with the word, I am going to enlist an expert to define it. That's coming later, but I am going to add a component to it for clarity. For this section I am incorporating the idea of *purpose* in with *passion*. Passion, as a definition, does exude an emotional element, more so than purpose. That is my rationale for opting for passion. And secondly, because we are using the model of Peter and what Jesus ignited in him, passion does tend to ascribe itself better to Peter's character.

So, all joking aside, let's get a definition. According to Townsend, passion is "focused desire." He goes on to give a fuller explanation:

> Passion is an emotion of great clarity. It is something you feel. You can talk about passion, and you can think about passion, but deep down, you feel it. It harnesses your interest and desire for something and points them in a specific direction.[11]

I like the way he defines the term passion, especially the last part, because that is what Jesus did with Peter. He reminded him of God's specific plan (remember Matthew 16), forgave and restored him, and gave him new direction, "To feed my sheep."

And that is what we see Peter doing from that point forward. His passion was now defined and it pointed him in a direction that was clear. The path was known now, and the journey clearly laid out. That was a big part of the puzzle for Peter, and once he had that clarity, there was no stopping him. That is a point that is often raised by many who see not just in Peter but in all the disciples a huge reversal.

Prior to the crucifixion they are a rabble lot. After the resurrection, nothing could stop them. The reality of what they represented ignited in them a passion that was unstoppable. Nothing could deter them from taking the message of Jesus to the whole world. That passion can inspire such motivation, despite my angst over the word, is something I hope every leader attempts to understand.

John Maxwell has an interesting way of proving the importance of passion. According to him, the people who enjoy the most success have this attribute, even though most of the time we look at credentials, education, work history and other factors. He quotes a survey which states:

- More than 50% of all CEO's of Fortune 500 companies had C or C-averages in college.

- Nearly 75% of all US presidents were in the bottom half of their school classes.

- More than 50% of all millionaire entrepreneurs never finished college.[12]

The defining factor was passion. I know it's a loaded term but I can state without hesitation from personal experience, that those who I know who have succeeded the most, just not in business but in life as well, are those who have found their burden, er, passion in life. Townsend helps us connect it further with the following:

Passion is ignited when the real self connects with the right task environment.[13]

I think this is the wonderful picture we get of Jesus with Peter. Shaping him for what God was preparing in him, and, at the right time, releasing him to fulfill the passion he had to serve Christ.

One final thought. I mentioned my angst with the term passion. One of the problems with passion is two-fold. First, it can become an obsession. You can be so dedicated to your work that you push yourself to excel to such degree that you eventually burn out. Or, a cause you are passionate about leads you to forget everything else-your health, your responsibilities, even your family. Remember, your strengths can become your liability.

Secondly, your passion can become forced upon others. One of the difficulties I've seen is when a person is judged because they do not hold the same degree of passion for a cause than another. It could be anything from abortion, government, prophecy…you name it, the list is endless.

For church leaders this can be seen in church budgets, where people who are passionate about a specific ministry will treat the value of the ministry based on its budget line. But as a leader, your responsibility is to lead the entire church, not one aspect of it, so decisions must reflect the whole, not just one group whose passion trumps all others.

This is why self-awareness is so important. It's another gage for tempering your passion so it does not become an obsession or toxin. So at this juncture, let me leave you with a few suggestions for practicing self-awareness in order to help guard you from impulsiveness. Some were given in Chapter 7, but here are a few more to consider:

- Remember the principle of the pause. Especially if you are a bit like Peter, and you find yourself getting in trouble with those you lead because of your impulsiveness. Find out what your triggers are-those situations that cause you to react inappropriately and find ways to identify them.

- Create a feedback loop. Find a trusted advisor or two, and allow them to give you candid feedback, especially in the areas where you know you struggle. With their help, create processes that play to your strengths and manage your weaknesses best.

- Record the decisions you make. Keep track of their progress. Did they result in the outcomes you expected? Why or why not?

- Find a coach who can help you with your inter-personal skills and presentation, especially if you think you are giving off the wrong impression. Have someone help you tune your ability to connect with others. A few years ago I hired a coach to help me present messages more effectively. It had nothing to do with handling of the text and everything on how to handle an audience; posture, tone, gestures, etc. It was incredibly helpful and productive. Though it wasn't specifically for interpersonal interactions, it did translate to one on one, as well as other areas like meetings, small groups, and similar settings.

A leader's self awareness can go a long way in preventing self-sabotage.

Impulsiveness can potentially become a Trojan Horse, and anytime you allow impulsiveness to diminish your capacity to lead from your strengths, it undermines your ability to lead well, or to lead at all.

CHAPTER 12

The Leadership Paradox

And remember, our Lord's patience gives people time to be saved. This is what our beloved brother Paul also wrote to you with the wisdom God gave him--speaking of these things in all of his letters. Some of his comments are hard to understand, and those who are ignorant and unstable have twisted his letters to mean something quite different, just as they do with other parts of Scripture. And this will result in their destruction. The apostle Peter writing about the apostle Paul in his letter of 2 Peter 3:15-16.

In any discussion about passion and faith, you cannot ignore the man Saul, who became the apostle Paul. His role in the formation of the early church has been debated for centuries: Was he the inventor of Christianity or was he part of the larger movement? Regardless, for his part, he has done more to shape Christianity than any other individual except Christ himself.

For his day and time, few rivaled the resume of the apostle Paul. Highly educated, socially connected, religiously passionate, he was an up and comer in the world of Judaism. He was so zealous for the faith that he became an ardent vigilante against the new sect of Christ followers.

His desire to guard Judaism made him a violent man. He was there at the stoning of Stephen in Acts 7. He actively sought to punish the believers (known as followers of the Way), but here is a description from Paul himself:

> I am a Jew, born in Tarsus, a city in Cilicia, and I was brought up and educated here in Jerusalem under Gamaliel. As his student, I was carefully trained in our Jewish laws and customs. I became very zealous to honor God in everything I did, just like all of you today. And I persecuted the followers of the Way, hounding some to death, arresting both men and women and throwing them in prison. The high priest and the whole council of elders can testify that this is so. For I received letters from them to our Jewish brothers in Damascus, authorizing me to bring the Christians from there to Jerusalem, in chains, to be punished. (Acts 22:3-5)

Paul, in his commitment to Judaism felt that he was honoring God. The violence he exacted on believers was justified in his mind as protecting the truth from this radical new cult. We can't miss the type of man Paul was. He describes himself as "very zealous." The Merriam-Webster dictionary defines zealous as "marked by fervent partisanship for a person, a cause, or an ideal."

Apart from the dictionary definition, I like looking the word up in a thesaurus as well, because often, that is where we find context more helpful for understanding the word. Here is what the thesaurus has for the word zealous:

> Fervent, ardent, fervid, fanatical, passionate, impassioned, devout, devoted, committed, dedicated, hard-core, enthusiastic, eager, keen, over-keen, avid, card-carrying, vigorous, energetic, intense, fierce.

Paul, by his own definition, is a pretty intense guy about what he believes and how it shapes his life. He's a man of action, who is eager to be a part of making things right, at least in his mind, as opposed to just sitting back and doing nothing.

But after an encounter with Christ on the Damascus Road in Acts 9, Paul was miraculously converted into a "Follower of the Way." What we see in the life of Paul is a shift, but a shift in two areas of his life that is significant to understand.

First is the shift in his core belief. Rather than seeing Christianity as the enemy, he now sees it as the truth: Jesus is the long-awaited Messiah and the Old Testament points to him. Salvation is found in him alone and the entire world needs to hear that message.

Secondly, Paul moves from being a violent man looking to exact punishment and death upon others, to being the target of punishment and death threats himself. If you study his life, Paul spends much of his Christian experience in prisons for the very belief he started out to destroy.

What is important to keep in mind is that the same zealous Paul before his conversion, is the same zealous Paul after his conversion. Apart from the two significant differences above, his characteristic make-up is essentially the same. The zealousness he exhibits has now been redirected.

The Title We Adopt

Have you ever asked someone to describe themselves? Most will struggle with it. Now ask them to describe themselves in one sentence, something that encapsulates who they believe they are, in a single phrase. Chances are you will get a lot of hemming and hawing.

Paul gave quite a bit of detail concerning his life, beliefs, the people he was with, the travels that he took. We also know a lot of personal things about him. However, Paul had one phrase that he used to identify the core of who he was. If you are able, like Paul, to succinctly frame your life in one sentence, you are able to give people a clear picture of what is your purpose and passion for living. He did use the term apostle, yes, which had title and authority attached to it. But there was one phrase he used that was more personal and self-revealing.

I'm alluding to Paul's repeated usage of the phrase, "Slave for Jesus Christ."[1] Some versions use the term servant, the Greek can mean either, but I like the tension that slave creates, a tension that Paul intended to show. It is presented as his overall stance, one in contrast to the life he held previously. I believe that Paul is aligning with Peter's thoughts. In Peter's second letter he is attacking false teachers and states in 2:19 concerning them:

> They promise freedom, but they themselves are slaves of sin and corruption. For you are a slave to whatever controls you. (2Pe 2:19)

The last sentence is important, because it helps us understand why the early apostles did not hesitate to categorize themselves as slaves. Peter did it, James did it, Jude did it.[2] They understand a reality of life that many of us want to ignore. Freedom is really an elusive prize because we are all a slave to something. No one is truly free. We are either a slave to ourselves, which is slavery to sin according to the Bible, or you are a slave to God. And the paradox is this, to be a slave to God, is to truly be free.[3]

For leaders of the early church, freedom was found only as a slave to Jesus. Anything else was slavery to a false freedom-a prison of our own making and design. I point out this distinction because it does impose upon Paul a framework not only for his life, but for his leadership as well.

It would therefore be fair to say that Paul's self-identification as a "slave of Jesus Christ" was the way he defined himself. Under that was all his core values, principles for life, convictions, ethics, morals, and sense of worth, something that every leader needs at their core.

I've known leaders who have a hero, someone they admire, or someone they long to emulate. Sometimes it's a parent or a peer in their industry. Those we admire deeply impact in ways that cause us to model ourselves after them and even adopt some of their values. For leaders in the church world, the matter of self-identity should be an easy one. Yet, we can forget that we have a model in Christ.

Without an ability to define your core, it can become easier to succumb to self-sabotage because there are no values inherent in your life that serve as guardrails against them. Your strengths are just that, your strengths and nothing more. They may give you enjoyment and work satisfaction, but they aren't imbued with values underneath them. The vacuum that leaves will someday be threatened by a weakness that will attempt to fill it.

We will deal further with this in the next chapter, but for now I want to show how Paul's ability to define his core serves as the heart of his passion. We treat Paul primarily as a theologian, evangelist, and church planter. Yet he was also a leader. And I want to dig a little deeper into the way he adopts his core value of being a "slave for Christ."

Since Paul is clear about his identity, the "who" question, it first and foremost defines the type of leader he is to be. One passage that models this well is found in 1 Corinthians 9:19-27. This is one of the best passages for understanding the mind, heart, passion, and motivation of this incredible leader:

> Even though I am a free man with no master, I have become a slave to all people to bring many to Christ. When I was with the Jews, I lived like a Jew to bring the Jews to Christ. When I was with those who follow the Jewish law, I too lived under that law. Even though I am

not subject to the law, I did this so I could bring to Christ those who are under the law. When I am with the Gentiles who do not follow the Jewish law, I too live apart from that law so I can bring them to Christ. But I do not ignore the law of God; I obey the law of Christ. When I am with those who are weak, I share their weakness, for I want to bring the weak to Christ. Yes, I try to find common ground with everyone, doing everything I can to save some. I do everything to spread the Good News and share in its blessings. Don't you realize that in a race everyone runs, but only one person gets the prize? So run to win! All athletes are disciplined in their training. They do it to win a prize that will fade away, but we do it for an eternal prize. So I run with purpose in every step. I am not just shadowboxing. I discipline my body like an athlete, training it to do what it should. Otherwise, I fear that after preaching to others I myself might be disqualified. (1 Corinthians 9:19-27)

From this passage, Paul demonstrates how his understanding of being a "slave" shapes his leadership. To bring this down in a simple way let's see how many questions get answered from this passage.

- Who? Because Paul is a slave for Christ, He has become a slave to all people (vs. 19). He then gives two examples by contrasting two different groups (the Jews and the Greeks, 20-21), and to those who are weak (22)

- How? Whether he's with the Jews, the Greeks, or the weak, Paul adapts himself to the context he is in (20-22). He sees himself as a servant to all because he is a slave to Christ.

- Why? Because he attempts to find common ground with all, he does all that he can to win as many to faith in Christ as he can. (19, 20-23)

- When and Where? Based on the athletic picture that Paul paints in verses 24-27 the answers to these two questions are anywhere and anytime. Paul's whole point is that he wants to win this race, to never let his guard down and be ready for every opportunity that comes his way.

How many of us can define our leadership in such a concise way. In this one passage, Paul can articulate what motivates him, what goals he has set, what defines his methods, and even the thing he fears if he doesn't follow through with his burden.

I think it is one of the key reasons God was able to use him in such a powerful way. Paul was determined and resolute. His strengths lay in clearly understanding who he was and who he belonged to. Prior to Paul converting to Christianity he was filled with raw potential. Though it was misguided, God took that raw material and re-directed it for his plan and purpose. And the world has never been the same.

Dark Passengers and Other Figures Lurking in the Shadows

Why did I take you through Paul's personal adoption of the slavery motif? For one, to help you understand what framed the life of this incredible man of God. Secondly, to also bring to bear the struggles he had as a leader, struggles that we assume to be only external. Paul endured many hardships-beatings, prison, lashings, shipwrecks, stoning, hunger, thirst, exposure, sleeplessness, and on and on (see 2 Corinthians 11).

In some ways we can understand the hardships that Paul faced. The first century was not kind to the new faith that was taking the known world by storm. When we read the accounts of Paul, he's well aware his life will be difficult as a Follower of the Way. But there is one struggle that defies all others, and was the most difficult hardship of all.

It appears in 2 Corinthians 12. In 12:1–6, Paul describes a remarkable spiritual experience he had 14 years before, in which he was "caught up" into what he calls the third heaven and given insight into spiritual realities. He was writing to the Corinthian church which was an experientially oriented church; they craved visions and voices and ecstatic spiritual experiences.

Many other teachers in Corinth claimed such experiences as their credentials for ministry. In response, Paul reminds the church that he was having ecstatic experiences when they were still in spiritual diapers. However, instead of boasting in his experiences, Paul chooses to boast about his weaknesses and infirmities. It begins in verse 7.

> So to keep me from becoming proud, I was given a thorn in my flesh, a messenger from Satan to torment me and keep me from becoming proud. Three different times I begged the Lord to take it away. Each time he said, "My grace is all you need. My power works best in weakness." So now I am glad to boast about my weaknesses, so that the power of Christ can work through me. That's why I take pleasure in my weaknesses, and in the insults, hardships, persecutions, and troubles that I suffer for Christ. For when I am weak, then I am strong. (2 Corinthians 12:7-10)

For the purposes of this book, this is an incredibly important passage. Paul was a key figure in the growth of the Christian church in the first century. His mark in history cannot be denied. Few in the time since can compare with the dedication of this man and the contribution he's brought to the world.

We are told he was given a "thorn in the flesh." This is a well known passage that has given scholars over the years plenty of opportunities to debate what Paul's "thorn in the flesh" was. There has been much speculation about what Paul means by it. The word we translate as "thorn" could just as accurately be translated "stake" or "spear." The word was used to describe a sharp instrument that caused pain, lodged deeply, and was difficult to remove.

Whatever it was, the "thorn in the flesh" was not a minor annoyance; it was not just a "pain in the neck." Rather, it was a chronic source of pain and anguish, so debilitating that it hindered his ability to serve Christ. Now, that is not what you want to hear from one of your star players. Every sport nut knows the anxiety that comes when a team's star player is hurt.

But here is the skinny on this passage. We've wasted more ink on trying to figure out the "thorn in the flesh" than God ever intended us to. God never wanted to define it, Paul never wanted to reveal it. I would contend this is one of those passages where we cannot see the proverbial "forest for the trees."

This is a classic example of asking a biblical text a question it was never meant to answer. The point of the passage, is whatever this "thorn" was, it was given to keep Paul from becoming prideful, conceited, arrogant … full of hubris! Does any of that sound familiar?

And here is an important reason why there are passages in the Bible like this one where something is not defined. We as humans have a tendency to find an "out" whenever we can. If Paul had mentioned the "thorn" being bad eyesight, for instance, we would treat those with bad eyesight as potentially being judged by God because of their pride. At the same time we might ignore real pride in our own lives because it doesn't match what Paul had.

It is left unknown intentionally, so we take to heart the essence of the passage. Not to allow pride to overtake our dependency on Christ. A lesson that needed to be taught to someone as dedicated to God as the apostle Paul. A lesson so important because of the leadership role he played in the development of the early church.

Paul was given incredible authority, power, and revelations. But he was also human. God wanted to protect his prized disciple from the one potential threat that was lurking in his heart-the threat of pride. I've said before that any leader worth their salt, someone worthy to follow, will naturally struggle with pride if they do not guard their character with humility.

God must have seen some potential danger in Paul to allow this "thorn" into his life, a thorn delivered by one of Satan's own messengers. And Paul prayed three times. I'm jolted by that acknowledgment. This man prayed with power, raising the dead, performing miracles, healing others. And yet, a prayer for himself is denied.

The language in the Greek is strong. Paul is pleading with God to take it away. There is active and fervent prayer to take whatever this thing was and to remove it from his life because Paul is tormented by it. And the response in each case is the same, "My grace is all you need. My power works best in weakness."

For any Christian leader, the strength you exhibit first and foremost, is the strength of Christ that empowers you to accomplish his will. It's the Spirit of God actively working through what you surrender to him that makes you strong.

The other lesson it teaches is that of dependence. We can so easily get into the whirlwind of activity and lose our sense of dependence on God. Paul recognizes that our weaknesses remind us of our need to depend on Christ, not on our own strengths and abilities alone.

As we said before, it is in our failures and our afflictions where our greatest lessons come. God does not want to keep us weak for weakness sake, but for dependency sake. What's your "thorn in the flesh?" What personal weakness or vulnerability causes you pain or hinders your ability to serve Christ freely and effectively? Maybe it's something obvious; maybe it's something no one would ever guess.

It could be something you've lived with for a long time or something that's happened to you more recently. Some thorns are more painful and debilitating than others, but we all deal with something.

We've all got disabilities of some sort.

Do we not love the stories of those who have overcome great difficulties and still managed to make the best of life? Why is it that we assume that those who succeed had an easy trip to the top? I like what Kent and Barbara Hughes write:

> That weakness brings strength is one of the great paradoxes of the Christian experience! G. K. Chesterton once described a paradox as "truth standing on its head crying for attention." …Those of us in ministry need to embrace this paradox. For the men and women God has used have always lived with the reality that they are merely clay. When they saw Jesus Christ, they became unconscious of all they used to call their wisdom and strength. And rather than focus on their weakness, they made it their business to open wide for all his treasure. From this flowed the surpassing greatness of his power. Ordinary Andrews became vehicles for the extraordinary. There is glory in the ordinary.[4]

Paul has inspired insights on the topic of leadership, especially concerning the matter of strengths and weaknesses. He raises it in a couple of key writings, as if he is acutely aware of the problem of self-sabotage. For all his theological mastery, Paul has a keen understanding of the practical side of doctrine. That belief shapes and informs our conduct. Of his thirteen letters, each contains examples of right living that proceeds from the basis of the theology he presents.

God in essence was saying to Paul that God needs to keep him weak in order that God's power can be shown more fully in Paul. For God's power to shine through it needs a vessel of weakness to work through. We love to talk about the life of Jesus, and how in a few short years all of history was touched by his life and death. His life though, is an amazing paradox of weakness that demonstrated to the world the true power of God.

On the practical side is the fact that an unguarded strength has the potential to hurt your faith more than a guarded weakness. As in Paul's case, God had to protect him from the very things God had blessed him with. God, who gives us all our gifts and abilities, intends for us to use them for his glory. Remember Solomon, who used the gift of wisdom for personal gain and pleasure.

When we take those gifts and use them selfishly for ourselves, we invite the potential for derailment. The irony is that the very gifts that God gives us can be the very gifts that cause us to discount God. Paul was given incredible power, authority, and revelation. If he for a second thought that the church was exploding across the Mediterranean because of his skill, then pride would already have been in his heart.

God was protecting him from the potential danger of such thinking. Conversely, we have no trouble acknowledging our weaknesses, at least to ourselves. We tend to seek help in the areas we struggle most. We may even pray for God's help and direction and enlist the support of those closest to us.

Frankly, weaknesses are easy to figure out most of the time. It normally takes some degree of honesty with yourself. So those areas are usually acknowledged if not outright guarded. But our strengths are another matter altogether. Since they give us satisfaction and are the easy part of our personality, we do not even think of protecting that part of us.

I would also argue these are where the Devil really wants to attack you. It's easy to drag you down in the area where you are weak. An addiction, a depression, a sense of guilt, a feeling of loneliness, the reasons are many. You can even be extremely productive at work but an utter wreck at home. You can be celebrated on the stage but incredibly alone when the spotlight is gone.

This can be especially hard for church leaders. Leadership in today's church is extremely difficult because you are expected to be a master at everything. What this can actually do is create great insecurity in a leader because it's impossible for one person to be gifted in every area. But the expectations today are that high.

And because we are church leaders, the attacks from the Evil One are never far off. Whatever weakness you may have will invariably be the easiest target. Make no mistake. His desire is to utterly destroy you by making you ineffective and irrelevant. He doesn't care if he takes you down with one of your weaknesses or better yet, one of your strengths.

In fact, I would say he doesn't even care about your faith. Your faith can be perfectly intact, but your effectiveness gone. If the devil can't derail your faith, the next best thing is to derail your ability to make a difference for God. That is not an outcome any faithful leader wants.

I have chosen intentionally not to look at 1 and 2 Timothy or Titus, books that normally come to mind when the subject of leadership is raised in the church. Though they are of value, my purpose has been to show Paul's sensitivity to the harnessing of our strengths for the right reasons and intent, something that was personal in his life as seen in 1 Corinthians. In the pastoral epistles his instructions are more didactic concerning leadership in the church. In any event, we learn from Paul that when we serve for the purpose of Christ his power is evident through us.

Looking Back to See Ahead

Beginning in chapter 10 of 1 Corinthians, Paul relates a brief history of Israel and their problem with idolatry. Not only does he mention the worship of idols, but also the practice of immorality. These are both themes we covered earlier. Paul identifies these two areas once again as being fraught with the dangers of infidelity.

> If you think you are standing strong, be careful not to fall. The temptations in your life are no different from what others experience. And God is faithful. He will not allow the temptation to be more than you can stand. When you are tempted, he will show you a way out so that you can endure. (1 Corinthians 10:12-13)

As we close out this section I want to take a moment to discuss this passage in the light of leadership. Paul begins with a simple enough warning: "If you think you are standing strong …" One of the arguments I've made throughout is the inherent danger in our strengths. Our successes can make us have a false sense of security.

I remember when I was a church planter some years back. We were in an area that was upper middle class. One of the more common push backs I got from people was that they did not need God because their lives were proof of his blessing. They would point at their home, their two cars, their cottage up north, or a plethora of other material advantages as proof of God's blessing. There was this false notion of being okay based on what they had.

Israel was guilty of the same thing. They had the miracles and the revelation of God but ended up worshipping idols and falling into immorality. The point that Paul is stressing is clear. Don't ever drop your guard, because you never know where the attacks will come from.

What's worse, this is where the door to self-sabotage can be opened. We want to harness our strengths for God's glory, but if we believe we have nothing to worry about, we are only deceiving ourselves. Remember, Paul goes on further to say we are all tempted equally. It's a reality in everyone's life.

I've already spent much time on the topic of temptation but want to add a couple of remarks. When it comes to the human trials common to this life, God is faithful. Based on this passage he has pledged not to test you beyond what you can bear, and also to provide a way out.[5]

Paul's point is that in ordinary human trials, we can expect divine help. We may have to endure for a time before the end is realized, but God is faithful to provide the "end" to a test that he didn't necessarily originate, but allowed. The concern and thrust is the encouragement to flee from idolatry.[6]

We live in a culture that celebrates rampant individualism, the very thing that hampers our ability to fully experience God's power. Our strengths are the last part of ourselves that we surrender and they are the one place we feel the most blessed by God. They are also the place where we are weakest in defending.

Our weaknesses compromise the majority of our prayers. I rarely hear someone pray, "Lord, protect me from the ability to make money. I just have this gift where I can make it grow easily, but I know it can become a problem." Or, "Lord, allow me to experience one setback. My business is growing so rapidly I'm afraid I'm going to feel it's all my doing. Give me something to keep me dependent on you and not to allow a sliver of pride to enter my heart."

I can honestly say I have not heard many of those prayers. Our strengths potentially become our biggest spiritual liability. God is unable to work when we are unwilling to surrender all of ourselves to Him. God is unable to fill us if we are already full of ourselves. Frederick Buechner wrote[7];

The trouble with steeling yourself against the harshness of reality is that the same steel that secures your life against being destroyed secures your life also against being opened up and transformed by the holy power that life itself comes from.

We have observed some key figures from the Scriptures with a particular view to their strengths and weaknesses. In concluding our character studies and before entering the final section, I want to give a bit of a recap concerning the observations we've made.

1. We began with Abraham. A man who was considered a friend of God and the father of faith. His life is epitomized by his trust in God, to the degree that he left his homeland to wander west under God's direction. But fear became his Trojan Horse, and this man of faith and trust allowed fear to undermine that faith, demonstrating a lack of trust in God.

2. Then there was Moses, the man God used to free a nation from slavery and to lead them through the wilderness. The man of the Ten Commandments and the Law who spoke face to face with God on the mountain. He taught a nation how to worship the Lord in holiness as he led them to the Promised Land. But anger was Moses' Trojan Horse. As a result of his act of irreverence towards God, Moses, the man who personified the Law, was not able to enter the Promised Land.

3. David was renowned for his faith in God. His purity and integrity gave him a reputation as a "man after God's own heart." He slew a giant, consolidated a nation, and created one of the most endearing books of the Bible; The Psalms. Yet David's Trojan Horse was pride, something that he struggled with all his days. The man of purity committed adultery and murder, spiraling his entire family into hatred and dysfunction for the remainder of his life.

4. Solomon was dubbed the wisest man on earth. His wisdom was renowned throughout the nations and his skill as an admin-

istrator was unparalleled. He wrote and collated the Biblical wisdom books and gave us some of the greatest philosophical works the world has known. But Solomon's Trojan Horse was infidelity, and acted in direct defiance of God's commands. This wise man became foolish. God judged him harshly and divided the kingdom after his death.

5. Peter was a disciple of Jesus. A man chosen, yet rash on almost every front. Consistently he either spoke or did something that caused him to be chastised by Jesus, yet at the same time he demonstrated great potential. Peter's Trojan Horse was his impulsiveness. In a moment of impetuousness, he promised to follow Jesus to death, but denied him when the moment of truth came. Though Peter experienced an epic failure, Jesus restored him and forgave him, which shaped Peter from that moment on to become the rock of the early church.

6. Paul was our last study. He demonstrated a zeal that at first made him an enemy of Christ. A miraculous intervention transformed him into the apostle to the Gentiles and he became history's pre-eminent church planter. He was given much power, authority, and revelation, but alongside those God gave him a "thorn in the flesh" to guard him from the potential of pride. Paul is different from the others in our study, but his life as a prominent leader shows a concern for the human strengths that can undermine the work of a man even as committed as he was.

Each of these areas of focus have taken the time to look at the place of strengths and weaknesses in our lives and learn valuable lessons. In each case we've seen the fallout of self-sabotage. Individuals who lived for God, yet fell in some way or another. And more interestingly, fell in the area of their greatest strength, demonstrating the fine line between faith and falling.

CHAPTER 13

A Text Outside of Its Context...

Be careful the environment you choose for it will shape you; be careful the friends you choose for you will become like them. - W. Clement Stone

Some years ago I heard a conference speaker say, "A text outside of its context leaves you with a con."[1] To some it may seem a trite saying but its truth cannot be denied. Our interpretation of what we read should have at least some awareness of its context, otherwise we can be guilty of misrepresenting the text. I've not only remembered this catchy phrase but have repeated it countless times in class and during messages. It's a principle I teach again and again.

Here is the sad reality: If I wanted, I could make the Bible say virtually anything. I can find support for murder, multiple wives, racial segregation, you name it. Whatever particular issue resonates with me it is easy to manipulate texts that will support my individual bent. The more we isolate a text from its historical, literary, and theological context, the more we can make it say whatever we want.

It is not an easy discipline to achieve because it takes work. You've got to get into the text and do the hard work of connecting the flow of the argument so you understand the essence of what is being taught. We hear this all the time when celebrities complain when a journalist has misquoted or taken a statement out of context. And in our world of gross de-contextualization, we can make anyone appear to say virtually anything.

A Leader Outside of Their Context...

What is true about interpreting the Bible in context is also true of leadership. Leadership, for the most part, is meant to be exercised within a particular sphere or context. For a leader, our unawareness of that context can render our particular strengths useless.

I think it's fair to say that many strong leaders carry their strengths into every area of life. After all how do you turn-on and turn-off the way you are naturally wired? If you have a job that demands precision and detail, you likely will exhibit that at home as well.

I remember a few years ago when our entire Board of Directors went to a seminar on effective Boards. One of the points that stood out for me is that a Board member does not have authority to act on behalf of the Board outside a duly appointed Board meeting, unless granted permission from the Board.

But how many times will a Board member exercise authority beyond the Board Room? Worse still, are those who in a social setting hear a Board member give an opinion, and go on to assume it is the opinion of the entire Board.

This illustration shows how even one board member, acting outside of their authority, can create disharmony and disunity. The Board should be a strong area of an organization, but if it doesn't conduct itself well, or there are deals and gossip happening outside of meetings, or there is constant infighting, the Board is sabotaging its effectiveness.

Context is a means by which our strengths are allowed to flourish in the environment they were meant to work best in. Remember when we said passion is ignited when the real self connects with the right task environment.[2] This is the best of both worlds, when your strengths match the context.

In discussing context we are talking about a number of factors:

- Environment - The areas where your strengths are meant to be used.

- Amount - The degree in which you bring your strength to a situation.

- Timing - The time(s) when your strengths make you most productive.

The debate in the business world continues on the definitions of strengths and where weaknesses play a role. That may be fine for the marketplace but I'm not sure it's entirely helpful in the church world. I gave you a definition that I was working on at the beginning and want to restate it here:

A true strength is whatever you are good at naturally that gives you energy, a sense of purpose, inherently motivates and inspires you. It is something that others see in you and want to emulate or follow.

Can I work with that definition a moment? Remember the Trojans? They were a strong and proud nation. Excavations of the site have shown that during the time of the proposed war the city was at its zenith.[3] Their sense of national pride and fidelity to their state would be their strength, something that would give their people a collective sense of purpose and meaning. It would unify them as a nation and validate their need to defend themselves against the Greeks.

Strengths, therefore, are not just on an individual level but on a corporate, institutional, and national level. There are many organizations that are known for their collective strengths and we easily identify not just with their products, but often with what they stand for. The art of branding is a prominent feature in many companies and institutions today.

There is one other note I need to make about the definition above. It assumes that whenever you are operating in your strengths you are naturally producing. You are able to execute effectively and see results when exercising them. Beyond giving yourself a sense of purpose and work, it transfers itself to giving meaning to the work you are engaged in because it is part of your strength matrix.

Back to context. Let's look at the church world and spiritual gifts.[4] These are given to every believer by the Spirit of God but they are essentially the strengths you bring to the rest of the body. Every person brings a strength to the church and every strength is meant for a particular context for the most part. This is essentially Paul's point when he writes:

Yes, the body has many different parts, not just one part. If the foot says, "I am not a part of the body because I am not a hand," that does not make it any less a part of the body. And if the ear says, "I am not part of the body because I am not an eye," would that make it any less a part of the body? If the whole body were an eye, how would you hear? Or if your whole body were an ear, how would you smell anything? But our bodies have many parts, and God has put each part just where he wants it. How strange a body would be if it had only one part! Yes, there are many parts, but only one body. The eye can never say to the hand, "I don't need you." The head can't say to the feet, "I don't need you." In fact, some parts of the body that seem weakest and least important are actually the most necessary. (1 Corinthians 12:14-22)

Paul is actually arguing for context here. Everyone has a gift (strength), that is meant to strengthen the body (community), and to be used in the place/ministry their strength was meant for (context).

As leaders we know what happens when someone is in a role or position that they should not be in. That is not to say they do not have a place, it's just they are in the wrong place.

Which goes back to a point I made some time ago, that one way to identify a person's gift is to look at what creates in them a sense of angst. For instance,

- Someone who's constantly frustrated by the condition of the kitchen at the church and wishes those in charge would get organized. They may have the gift of organization or hospitality.

- A person who is frustrated by the lack of funds for missions, may have the gift of outreach or evangelism.

- Someone who is continually frustrated by the plight of the poor-despite the limitation of resources to help everyone-may have the gift of empathy and compassion.

Oftentimes these points of frustration serve as a telltale marker of a strength. Likely due to the degree of passion that it evokes in the individual.

Which lends itself to our second point. Our strengths are easily identified by others. Ever been in a meeting and decided you needed someone to head up a new initiative and everyone thought of the same person? That's context. Your group may forward a few more names, but usually the list is based on the strengths you've identified in them. In the church world, a person's strength is never validated by the person alone, but by the community, because the strength is meant for the community in the first place, not just for the individual with the strength.

We've seen context become a problem outside the church too.

1. A lawyer who is skilled at argumentation and seeing black and

white, but struggles in relationships because it's not about winning arguments and most relational situations tend to be grey.

2. An accountant who can decipher every digit and balance pages of numbers at work but is so tied to the numbers that he is incredibly frugal to the point that his family never experiences life beyond a particular budget line.

3. A health addict whose lifestyle habits are the epitome of discipline, proper nutrition, and exercise, but exasperates everyone close because of the constant berating they receive due to what they eat and how they look.

These are just some examples of the problems we can face when are strengths are used outside the context of their greatest usefulness. It's not that a work strength is totally useless in a home environment and vice versa, but it may need to be tempered in a way to suit the different conditions. This is similar to Collins who writes about getting the right people on the right seats on the right bus.[5]

In one blog post by Robert Kaiser and Robert Kaplan for Harvard Business Review, they stress the need for leaders to be aware of their situation, that it is helpful for leaders to think of adjusting their strengths like a volume control. They claim that it will require a deft touch, which I see as a case for self-awareness, and equal parts knowing your strength and knowing your audience (again, context).[6]

For leaders then, the tension of self-awareness and contextual awareness becomes a real test of the way you utilize your strengths. And how they are perceived. As noted in some of our biblical stories, Abraham did not appear very trusting of God when he was lying to save his bacon.

How wise would Solomon have appeared to faithful Israelites

who witnessed him sacrificing on the altar of a pagan god? They would have instantly questioned the veracity of his faith, if not the claim of wisdom he was reputed to exemplify.

Harnessing the Entire Package

In every organization there is a tension between character and competency. For the most part, the tendency is to zero in on competency, at the expense of character. We can lean into satisfying the job description which is primarily oriented towards tasks and what a person can produce for the organization. I know these are gross generalizations but in this regard, the business world is motivated more by competency, as opposed to the character focus of the church world.[7]

A leader in the church world must first and foremost be a person of character. And as many writers before have stated, character determines capacity. As we've seen in our character studies, the matter of their personal make-up, the strengths they possessed, and the personal struggles they faced, all played contributing roles in whether they succeeded or failed.

Strengths in the business world may be more performance oriented, but in the church world the behaviors behind them are just as key. It may be acceptable in the marketplace to minimize your weaknesses, but not so in the spiritual world. Spiritual growth is a holistic, all-in enterprise.

Which is why I've kept to acknowledging strengths as a behavioral component of your make-up, and not just an analytical framework used to measure your output, productivity, or results. For us, it should be much more. Because in the church world, it's all about relationship with God, and our relationship with others.

So our strengths are a part of who God wired us to be, as much as our weaknesses are. We've argued, though, our strengths can also become our weaknesses, either directly, by abusing or overusing them, or by allowing a weakness to undermine the strength and debilitate it.

As humans, we have the propensity for self-sabotage. To self-destruct. I have seen this play out so often that no one could convince me otherwise. In fact, whenever I recognize the strengths inherent in another I can anticipate what the potential dark side could be.

It sounds a little predictive but I've seen the pattern too much to ignore. I've even talked to counsellors who claim to see it as well. And it's not that whatever strengths we have will always cause us to fail in that area, it's just that without self-awareness, it is probable.

Everyday we rub shoulders with people who have great strengths. And we've observed how they can sometimes have a dark side. Let me give you some examples and see if you recognize any of these people:

- You've met the person who is very talented at administration and oversight. Their function entails helping to give direction and recommendations. They are incredibly efficient and productive. But they are deeply insecure. Everything is fine until you disagree. In fact, over time, their insecurity becomes more evident and working with them just awkward. Each day you walk on eggshells because of the resentment you feel from them.
- You've met the analytical person who has to parse everything to its finest detail. They have great skill at dissecting each problem and related decision. But they question everything tediously and over time create an atmosphere of doubt and decision paralysis. Their incessant questioning of everything begins to sound like the annoying three-year-old who asks every five minutes that insatiable question "why".
- You've met the numbers guru who can look at a budget and make any line say virtually whatever he wants. They're adept as a financial analyst in their day job but create havoc for those less gifted. Especially when they disapprove of the way a budget is

being allocated. They have the ability to park on one figure and make you question the entire thing.

- You've met the creative mastermind, adept at all things artistic. Your organization has benefitted from their input and stylistic flare. But they are boorish and difficult to work with. They treat others as incompetent if they dare attempt anything creative and are slighted by the least bit of criticism.

- You've met the eternal optimist who sees the good in everyone and exhibits deep compassion for people. They are good at listening, showing mercy, and giving advice. Their primary concern is to make others happy. But they tend to be cowardly and overly sensitive themselves to criticism.

- You've met the person who does everything for their children. There isn't a single life experience that hasn't been directed or shared by the parent. The children want for nothing and the parent stands guard over their entire lives. At first you admire their sense of duty to their family until you realize that the kids cannot cope with the slightest problem and are in constant meltdown. The home is a continual theatre of drama. You come to see the parent as over-compensating for a childhood or love they believe they did not receive.

- You've met the myopic person. They have a passion for a particular project, department, ministry, or initiative. Their energy and focus is admirable to say the least, as is their conviction. But their hobby horse is just one piece of the entire institution, and they can never see beyond their niche to the detriment of the organization's health. In fact, if you allowed them an opportunity to set direction, they would derail the entire enterprise for their passion.

- You've met the person who appears to agree with everything. They nod in on every decision and even volunteer to work on specific parts to bring the project together. They are easy to work with and seem to get along with you and your way of doing things. Until you realize that they produce very little and in fact are negative about the organization behind your back. This passive-aggressive behavior makes you wonder where you really stand.

- You've met the person who demonstrates an incredible ability to be generous. They are usually tapped by everyone because they seem to have a never ending pot of resources and an inability to say no. They struggle with a too-impulsive character because they are undisciplined and irresponsible and their family is actually suffering because of it.

- You've met the person who is hyper-spiritual and seems to have a direct line to God. You admire their ability to pray with eloquence and the fact that they can discern the presence of the Spirit in any environment. But over time they seem to just get creepier, and you begin to feel uncomfortable in the way they see everything as a full out spiritual war.

Honestly, we've all known these people. We engage with them everyday, at work, at school, at church, and at home. Some of them are people we love dearly. We may even have married them because of a strength we saw. I've counseled many couples over the years, so I know that it's no secret that the very qualities you found so cute and endearing in the beginning are the potential grievances you will have about them thirty years later, maybe sooner. If you make it that long!

We not only know some of these people, they may even be us! My point with the examples above is not to ridicule, but to help us see that we all have the ability to let our individual behavioral strengths become a liability. A church is made up of people, broken people, imperfect people, and those just trying to manage life as best as they can. And so, certainly, a strength can be abused or overused when we consider the imperfect, fallible nature of people.

I want to make an observation about the examples given above. It has been my experience that there is a threshold. Here's what I mean by it. I've personally known some incredibly gifted leaders. At first, I admired them for their strengths, whatever they were. But of those who lacked self-awareness, either their insecurity, pride, arrogance, hubris (whatever it was), reared its ugly head more and more over time.

What I found at some point is you begin to no longer see their strengths as a value to the degree you did in the beginning. Their "dark side," as it were, takes centre stage more and more. When that happens you've entered the stage where a line has now been crossed. When you enter this stage, the statement you begin to hear in the back of your mind is this: *The cost of having this person is now outweighing the benefits.*

That is what I call the threshold moment. And as a leader it can be a difficult place to be, because if you are sensing this, you can be assured that others are sensing this as well. Which is why I believe a study and understanding of strengths is a valuable exercise for leaders.

Here's why: If you are cognizant of the strengths of your staff, team, whatever, you will also know the potential they may have for self-sabotage. Not that all will, but that they might. It's simply an awareness thing. And if you're sensitive to the potential downsides of their strengths, you can help them by sending them to training sessions or placing them with mentors who can work with them in those areas.

It's a very pro-active approach to developing your team for the betterment of everyone. We all stumble and fall from time to time, but wouldn't it be good to at least catch the warning signs as they appear?

We now live in a society that limits the types of direct questions you can ask during an interview process. That's a problem in the church world but there are lots of creative ways to get the information you need if you take the time to research new methods.

Nonetheless, one area that everyone has no trouble telling you in an interview is what their strengths are. Even personal ones. These are the times for bragging on their skill set. They may also be revealing to you their greatest area of struggle. I'm carefully listening when they begin to list the strengths and the benefits they will bring to the organization. It may be a clue to what you can expect in the future.

We hear continually that character should trump competency. Couldn't agree more. But in the beginning, in the process of hiring someone, your ability to see a person's character is limited. You can do background checks and talk to as many people who know them, creep their online profiles, talk to past employers, but in reality, these are usually dominoes lined up in preparation for your expected investigation.

So in a slightly modified version of character over competency is the threshold question. "What potential problems could we experience down the road based on what they tell us their strengths are?" "Where could their strengths cost us?" When we interview we attempt to look at character and a personality that will align itself with present team or staff. But you are also trying to find the right person with the right skill set for the position. I'm just saying to not ignore those skill sets as being potential problems for you in the future.

I remember in my late teens we had this new guitarist join our band. He was nothing short of amazing. He had the licks and solos down cold from every cover song we had in our repertoire. We sounded better than ever. Within months we couldn't get him out fast enough. He gave me a new appreciation for all the stories of ego-crazed artists I had heard. That was my first real lesson in looking beyond the skill.

A more difficult prospect is when you ask the threshold question of yourself: "Am I now costing the organization more than benefitting it?" It truly takes a person of deep conviction and character to be able to ask this of themselves and to answer with honesty. More often than not, a leader may look more to what they gain from their position as opposed to what they give.

I'm starting to see this as a good inventory exercise. As a leader who wants to leave a healthy legacy and to pass off the church I lead to better leaders, the question gains more relevance every year. It's never an easy exercise and it certainly brings to light areas of improvement.

Moving Towards the Light

People expect leaders to be omnipotent. We are far from it. In the busyness of our vocation we can quickly place disciplines of self-improvement aside for more pressing priorities. We've argued for the need to become more self-aware and to continue to hone this discipline throughout your life.

In order to become the most effective leader, your ability to respond to the challenges of your position is not purely dependent on your technical skills. Your depth of character will allow you to navigate those moments when conflict, stress, and unrealistic demands press you to the wall.

I'm convinced that the most direct route to improving any relationship immediately is humility. But humility should also be turned inward. In knowing who you are, what your default tendencies are, where you struggle and why, you are best able to protect yourself from self-sabotage.

However, getting a strength under control can be just as daunting. Since it is something that comes so naturally, we can become defensive if we are challenged about it. I've heard the response, "But I enjoy it so much," or, "It gives me a sense of satisfaction and accomplishment," whenever I've had to speak to someone about a behavior that needed to be curtailed.

Have you ever been guilty of these?

1. You are a good speaker and you need to influence a decision. Your tendency will be to talk more and listen less.

2. You have great visioning capacity but are guilty of running ahead of everyone and become frustrated when they're not keeping up.

3. You specialize in problem solving which is your real niche. You view everything as a problem to be solved when in reality they are just tensions to be managed. You may even create more problems by attempting to solve the original one.[8]

There are many vices that can contribute to a leader's self-sabotage. The current climate advocates strongly for strengths which is fine, but in the church world we need to be cautious. Two other dangers that lurk are those of compartmentalization and character creep.

It's easy for a leader to begin to compartmentalize their life. They pull out their skills and exercise their duties as needed. But the personal life is suffering. Many church leaders struggle with their family life because of the stress that ministry places on families. The bubble that the children and spouse live under can be a heavy burden to bear. I've been shocked over the years by the expectations that have been placed on my wife and kids.

Over time, the demands of work and the pressures of home can create problems between the two. Most leaders face it in some way or another. This can lead to feelings of inadequacy, vulnerability, fear, blame, you name it. The spiral can even lead to the potential for addiction and other personal problems. The leader's strengths can even be a contributor to their denial and in their refusal to admit their need for help. This can further lead to intense feelings of shame and guilt.

Since we've stated how our weaknesses can dismantle our strengths on the road to self-destruction a case in point is made by Brene Brown in her book, *The Gifts of Imperfection*.[9] I find some of her insights helpful when it comes to this subject, as she recounts her own journey from alcohol addiction to wholeness. As a researcher she has written perceptively on guilt, shame, and other like vices.

She states that our usual first response to vulnerability and pain is to not acknowledge them but attempt to numb them. To take the edge off as it were. This comes through many venues. She writes, "We can anesthetize with a whole bunch of stuff, including alcohol, drugs, food, sex, relationships, money, work, care-taking, gambling, staying busy, affairs, chaos, shopping, planning, perfectionism, constant change, and the internet."[10]

After many years of research she believes that we all attempt to take the edge off, to find a way to numb ourselves from the fear we have of being vulnerable. When we attempt to numb the pain we derail opportunities to experience authenticity and honesty in who we are. Her most profound insight is given in this summary:

> In another very unexpected discovery, my research also taught me that there's no such thing as selective emotional numbing. There is a full spectrum of human emotions and *when we numb the dark we numb the light*. When I was "taking the edge off" of the pain and vulnerability, I was also unintentionally dulling my experiences of good feelings, like joy.[11]

I've italicized the phrase, … "when we numb the dark we numb the light." I have heard many times that your personal life is your own and has no bearing on your ability to lead. That may be true from a purely pragmatic view when a task has to be accomplished, but it's far from helpful to the leaders entire well-being.

I'm not sure how many leaders are numbing themselves in the dark, and not experiencing the full benefits of the light because they believe one does not affect the other. The tensions of home life are dulling their ability to lead at work and vice versa. And where one brings discouragement it robs the victories of their full import in the other. Or what if insecurity, fear, or an addiction plagues you in the dark, what effects can you imagine they will have in the light. I often wonder if this isn't one of the reasons joy is missing from many believers lives.

Brown goes on to say further,

Feelings of hopelessness, fear, blame, pain, discomfort, vulnerability, and disconnection sabotage resilience. The only experience that seems broad and fierce enough to combat a list like that is the belief that we're all in this together and that something greater than us has the capacity to bring love and compassion into our lives.[12]

She goes on to affirm the need for spirituality. Imagine that, a researcher here acknowledging the importance of living a life of self-aware vulnerability that makes us accountable to something greater! If you are a leader in the church world, this should give you pause, especially as we seek to live faithfully as Followers of Christ and to the calling of the Kingdom.

Leaders, have a tendency to hide behind their strengths. They can become a barrier to authenticity and vulnerability. They can cause you to numb areas of your life, inevitably numbing the good parts too. Take the lists in previous chapters on becoming self-aware and put them into practice and find help if needed. You cannot afford to let yourself continue on the path you're on.

That is the danger when leaders become isolated and insulated. A second is when you allow your character to be eroded little by little. If you're intent on personal improvement then character becomes a work in progress. It is built by every decision and choice you make. It can erode in the same way. We rarely take an inventory of the choices we've made and chart where they have led until it's too late. Ralph Waldo Emerson put it well: "The force of character is cumulative."[13]

But throughout the entire breadth of history stands witness after witness of the perils of leaders who take small steps of erosion to an eventual landslide of failure. What you begin to guard as it pertains to your character you never let up on. Remember the admonition to "guard your heart." Jim Collins explains how character erodes.

> A bit further along the continuum, we encounter the malleable masses. These were the people who, in the presence of an opportunity to behave differently, got drawn into it, one step after another. If you told them 10 years ahead of time, "Hey, let's cook the books and all get rich," they would never go along with it. But that's rarely how most people get drawn into activities that they later regret. When you are at step A, it feels inconceivable to jump all the way to step Z, if step Z involves something that is a total breach of your values. But if you go from step A to step B, then step B to step C, then step C to step D ... then some-day, you wake up and discover that you are at step Y, and the move to step Z comes about that much easier.[14]

Character erosion becomes a factor whenever our strengths work against us. We can fool ourselves into believing that we can manage the little indiscretions. A small transgression can easily be covered up. In my experience it is the strengths that we have that do most of the internal talking when you are personally faced with a decision to move from A to B. The importance of taking intentional inventory of your decisions and weighing them against your values, is one way to counter the ever looming potential of character creep.

As we move into the closing chapter let me encourage you to continue to assess your leadership in a full 360 degree evaluation. Embracing not only your weaknesses but identifying the potential that even your strengths have in diminishing your ability to lead effectively.

CHAPTER 14

Protecting the Leader in You

Leadership is character in action - Warren Bennis

"The nobility and the fragility of the human being. The distance between the two traits is not that great." - Donald Keough.

We began with the well known story of the Trojan War. A war that ended primarily because the pride of the Trojans was elevated, thus blinding them to the dangers the horse held inside. That misstep not only cost them the war, but the burning of their city and the massacre that took many Trojan lives. Their only fault was believing the Greeks had left.

Our propensity to self-destruct and self-sabotage can lead us into similar consequences. They may not always be as dramatic or substantial as the Trojan War, but for many, the consequences are just as significant. That is why the subject of leadership continues to gain so much attention, because leaders affect so many lives on a daily basis. In most institutions, as the leadership goes, so goes the entire organization. As Tim Irwin reminds us,

"Deficits in authenticity, humility, self-management, and courage become more dangerous as we take on more leadership, and can cause us to ignore glaring signals that might otherwise save us from cata-strophic demise."[1]

Whenever we experience the failure of a leader, in any enterprise, whether sacred or secular, the world is diminished. Every time I hear of a prominent leader's failure, my first reaction is not to point fingers, but to grieve for the many faithful leaders who could lose some influence because of it. Secondly, I pray that the fallen leader will learn from their fall.

I believe in leaders, and I also believe they are the ones who shape the world for significant change. Leadership is that important. It's that conviction which compelled me to put the effort into this work. I've also been intentional in the area of focus. My intent was not to write a treatise about leadership in terms of definition, nature of Christian leadership, facets of our calling, nature of empowerment, or even the scope of our mission.

There are many books far more erudite on the subject. My purpose was to weigh in on the strengths versus weaknesses component of leadership through the lens of certain biblical characters. To me, this was an important exercise because it placed these stalwarts of the faith precisely into their human context. A context that many forget to preview before launching into their theological high-mindedness.

The failures we witnessed in the lives of Abraham, Moses, David, Solomon, Peter, and Paul (although his case is somewhat different), are the same ones we mimic on a regular basis. But the factor that can-not be ignored in each of them is the place of God in their lives. The one constant throughout every success and failure they experienced.

Our lives are shaped by whatever or whoever we believe is in charge. As leaders in the church, our primary responsibility is to be a faithful Follower of Christ first, with everything else following from there. This is the easy part of who and what defines us as leaders. This part of the equation cannot be denied, nor should it ever be.

Throughout I have repeated a continual warning. Whether its fear, anger, infidelity, impulsiveness, or a host of other potential characteristics, they can act as a Trojan Horse to a leader. They can undermine the very strengths that make you successful. But the danger doesn't just end there. Those very strengths can furthermore become liabilities that cause you to self-sabotage. Either way, your leadership has been affected.

I want to repeat a statement that I've used to summarize each section that we've explored:

> Anytime you allow something to diminish your capacity to lead from your strengths, it undermines your ability to lead well, or to lead at all.

In light of this axiom, below is a list of the potential ways a strength can become a means for you to self-destruct.

The Mechanics of a Trojan Horse and How To Recognize a Potential Enemy.

1. With our strengths we feel okay, even untouchable. They are what give us confidence for meeting the challenges of life. They are the reason we succeed or advance to where we are.

2. Because they are a strength, our tendency is not to guard or protect them. They are the last place we would expect to be attacked. The best we do is cultivate them further, which builds a false confidence in them.

3. We tend to believe that our strengths will compensate for any weakness. But an unguarded strength is potentially more dangerous than a guarded weakness.

4. When we pray, we rarely petition God for protection against what is healthy, positive, or strong as opposed to what is negative, hurtful, or needful. Praying is a key to guarding your strengths.

5. Because they are a strength, we can tend to become arrogant and prideful with them and the abilities they give us. Therefore we don't anticipate failure as a direct result of them.

6. We can also become careless and thoughtless, especially the more talented and gifted we are. We can lose the ability to be attentive and lose our objectivity because of an overconfidence in our abilities. Again, this leaves us open to derailment.

7. Our strengths can make us feel invincible. So much so that in times when others are sensing the warnings, we are oblivious to them.

8. We lose the ability to learn well the lessons of failure. In fact, we may become so averse to failure that we never grow beyond the superficiality that our strengths can foster in us. Strengths in particular are best honed by the experience of failure.

9. We are the most vulnerable immediately after a victory, and more often than not, that victory has come as a result of exercising our strengths. Because of this, we are unaware of the depth of our exposure during that vulnerable time, which leaves us open to falling.

10. Our strengths can tempt us to believe that we do not need accountability, therefore isolating us from the very people or structures that would help protect us.

11. A strength outside of its context can end up becoming a weakness, because context is where a strength operates best.

12. Your greatest strengths can also be the greatest source of personal frustration. Because of this, you may exploit your strengths in ways that can be hurtful to others and harmful over all.

13. Lastly, our strengths can almost make us feel divine. The very gifts, strengths, and attributes that are divinely and gracefully given to us become the very things that cause us to deny our need for God altogether.

I am not going to say that this book will prevent you from ever sabotaging yourself and the people you lead, but my hope is that it will give you an awareness of what may be lurking around the corner. Great men of God had moments when they stumbled, but were able to rebound, learn from them and move on. And for all their failure, God still was able to accomplish incredible things through them, moving his plan forward.

It's not to say that failure and self-destructing are one and the same. You can have a failure as a leader (say the loss of an important contract), but not equate that to a moral self-destruct. Because as we've pointed out, failure, even those catastrophic ones, can lead to growth and learning as a leader if you allow it.

Leadership's most important role is best understood not as it relates to leading others, but in leading yourself. As John Maxwell writes,

> We commonly think of a leader's greatest victory as being over others, as defeating an opposing team or a rival business. However, as Plato wrote, "the first and best victory is to conquer self." Every leader faces a struggle against self-interestedness. Yet whereas followers tend to think of themselves first, leaders have learned to put others ahead of themselves.[2]

We've all heard the saying that if we fail to learn from history we are doomed to repeat it. When it comes to leadership failure, history has much to teach us. This should force us to pause and consider our own situation and circumstances. If better men and women have experienced failure, even through their strengths, then all the more need to be diligent. There are great lessons to be learned from the failures of others.

Your integrity as a leader depends on it. Those who you surround yourself with should help reinforce that integrity, not attempt to dismantle it. Otherwise, the progress towards failure may have already started. Do not overestimate your own strength. That's the benefit of learning from others because it helps you to realize that you could make the same mistakes.

I recently read, "Success does not change us; it only magnifies what has always existed inside of us." The author continues to flesh out his statement:

> See, when we start out, we have zero equity. With zero equity comes zero influence. No one has to put up with us because they have nothing to lose by blowing us off, and we usually have nothing to offer them that will improve their situation. Over time, our talent and creativity start to develop. We start to get a little better at what we do, and people notice. As people notice, we start to have more opportunity. When we dominate our new opportunities, we get more "successful." Now, the same people who would pay us little attention desire to get all of our attention.[3]

This is the leader's dilemma over time, that as our influence and accomplishments grow, the core of who we are gets more exposed and potentially more open to pride and arrogance, a glimpse of what was always there in the first place.

Jesus had harsh words for the religious leaders who were corrupt. Their strength was in the intense study and parsing of the Old Testament Scriptures and Law. And yet, they lived legalistic lives, expressing themselves in judgmental actions towards others with nary a thought to their own sins.

> You brood of snakes! How could evil men like you speak what is good and right? For whatever is in your heart determines what you say. A good person produces good things from the treasury of a good heart, and an evil person produces evil things from the treasury of an evil heart. (Matthew 12:34-35)

Strengths can become a blind spot then. And often, the sins we make the most excuses for, the ones we are most blind to and minimize, are the sins that have us most in their grip. This is a problem on an individual level for sure, but becomes amplified in the life of a leader. Because whatever is in your heart determines how you lead.

The Most Potent Trojan Horse

The Bible, through its stories and character insights, has much to teach us. Due in part to the fact that its stories serve as a mirror for us while at the same time a window into God. On the human side, both strengths and weaknesses are given their due in the lives of those who we read in its pages. On the divine side, God is given the worship he is due, his character remaining constant, holy, perfect, and above human frailty.

It's the intersection of the two that makes each story so personal and real. We see ourselves in the narratives, in the personal struggles of the people who wrestle amidst the frailties of the human spirit, driven by a divine task. God knows our strengths and weaknesses, yet despite their full revelation to him, entrusts us with his eternal work to move the world to a better place, according to his purposes. This is the true leader's calling in life.

Our position as leader comes primarily from God, while our

character determines our capacity to lead. It's in many ways a sacred trust and the investment takes a lifetime. Faithful leadership is under the auspices of God. As a church leader myself, and a student of leadership, I grow more convinced over time that we need to take our divine calling as seriously as possible. Far too much is happening around us and leadership committed to God and his purposes is needed more than ever.

My students are surprised when I tell them that I have little to no faith in humanity. It may be a bit of cynicism creeping in as I get older, but the premise is one I'm convinced of. I know there are many in our world who work with integrity of heart and purpose to alleviate the plight of others.

They are advocates for the poor, the homeless, the disenfranchised, the destitute. There are those fighting for justice and the protection of rights where there are none. Others commit each day to elevating the hope of the elderly and sick, and keep the will to continue in the forefront of their lives.

There are the brave and heroic who in times of crisis and tragedy move with courage into situations that would make others flee. And we can't forget the faithful who each and every day do their duties, whether in the home, work, or school, with diligence and perseverance.

There are many who do good and make the world we live in a better place. I dare not insult those who encourage us every day and I don't mean to. But I am talking about something much more important. Something that is losing its embrace in which I believe will eventually cause us great dismay. And that is our reliance upon God.

Here is what I am saying. If we believe in the power of the human spirit to overcome the problems we face on a continual basis, then history is a discouraging recording to re-play. Pessimistic, maybe? But in my mind, realistic. My proposition is that our hope in humanity triumphing is based on a false assumption, because we will never be able to lead beyond the capacity of what we worship. And if we worship human intelligence, ingenuity, and wisdom, then I believe we are in serious trouble.

To me, the dependency on our ability to make the "world a better place" is the ultimate Trojan Horse. Our pride and arrogance, in the face of God, will lead us to implode upon ourselves eventually. For all the good I see around me, the truth is, there are as many if not more disturbing trends happening as well. Some of those trends being nothing more than old evils being played out in different arenas with different players.

From politics, to health care, to gas prices, to human slavery, to taxation, to corruption, to murder, to theft; the list is endless. And again, I know there are people in the trenches trying to make a difference every day, but what of the systemic problems we continue to face generation after generation? That is why I believe in leadership that is God centered and focused, based on humility and serving others.

I think the most destructive Trojan Horse is to think we can collectively make the world better through human strength alone. I think it is the worst deception we could fall for and our fate will continue to be tenuous if that is where we place our hope.

Conversely, I am sympathetic to the many who will point an accusatory finger in the direction of religion. Nor will I for a moment defend the injustices of the past or even the present. Frankly, some of what is propagated in the name of Christianity leaves me grieving and at times angry. Because for some, these are the very reasons they've made their bed with human potential and not in God.

If truth be known, I am somewhat anxious for what I'm advocating here because to some, it will allow them to rationalize their legalistic, narrow-minded, hypocritical, and judgmental presentation of the Gospel, something I am adamantly against because of the harm it does to the witness of Jesus and what he died for. The very accusations and judgments we level against others are part of the reason Jesus got on that cross in the first place.

If you are a leader, whether in church or industry, my hope is that you will embrace real leadership-rooted in God, empowered by the Holy Spirit, with humility, service, and self-awareness as key tools in your arsenal. The world has had enough of self-centered, boisterous, power-mongers, and egotists whose entire existence defines hypocrisy to the letter.

Instead, the world longs for authentic leaders whose faith is in a God who loves them, motivated by a willingness to serve with joy. It won't alway be perfect, but it will be honest. It won't always be easy, but it will be worth it. It won't always change people's hearts, but it will leave a seed.

That is what we witness in the lives of the characters we studied. Human beings, who became leaders under God's charge. Leaders who in their time changed the world. Some of their stories are encased in times when violence permeated the earth, but are we any less violent today as we survey the world landscape.

What they did have in common was faith in God, and a desire to serve him in whatever way they could. They surrendered themselves and watched as God worked wonders through them. Their knowledge of the Holy One propelled them to lead with conviction, faith, and integrity. As we have hopefully demonstrated, their greatest failings came when they leaned more on their human strengths and potential, and for a time, experienced the consequences of those lapses in faith.

I've experienced the absolute worse and absolute best in my life as a leader. And frankly, the times that loomed darkest in my life were the times I veered closer to my own abilities rather than trusting God with his. After all, he is the one able to accomplish the impossible, but when reliance and faith have been placed wholly in his care, I have never been disappointed.

Lead like you mean it, with intent and purpose. Just make it God's not your own. Because God will make all the difference in your life, not just in your leadership. As many before can attest, God has done wondrous things, and he can do them through you if you release yourself from your own prison. God is the hero of every biblical story, and he can be the hero in yours.

Let me remind you again with this:

> Anytime you allow something to diminish your capacity to lead from your strengths, it undermines your ability to lead well, or to lead at all.

The greatest strength that you can have in your life is God, and his strength is never in danger of a Trojan Horse. He does not succumb to the frailties that will derail us. As we allow him to work in us, his strength will empower everything we do.

Become the leader God means for you to be and make a commitment to be shaped by his Spirit, not yours. I hope this book has been an encouragement to you, and as we close, I want to do so by looking again at a few verses from the foot washing in John 13. It describes the moment where Jesus did something so unexpected and dramatic that his disciples must have wondered what he was up to?

> So he got up from the table, took off his robe, wrapped a towel around his waist, and poured water into a basin. Then he began to wash the disciples' feet, drying them with the towel he had around him. (John 13:4-5)

In a moment of vulnerability, Jesus demonstrates the heart of leadership that has the power to transform the world around us. No one can deny the impact that Jesus has had throughout the centuries. Millions follow him to this day. The influence that Jesus has is undeniable.

I'm sure it is partly due to moments like this one in John 13, which demonstrated a definition of success that is counter-intuitive to the power models so prevalent throughout history. It had to have shocked the disciples that their Master was now stooping before them and performing such a menial task. But Jesus was not finished.

> And since I, your Lord and Teacher, have washed your feet, you ought to wash each other's feet. I have given you an example to follow. Do as I have done to you. I tell you the truth, slaves are not greater than their master. Nor is the messenger more important than the one who sends the message. Now that you know these things, God will bless you for doing them. (John 13:14-17)

The lesson he imparted to his disciples in that room set in motion a way of relating to others as leaders, that forever changed the course of history and the way leadership is defined. To serve others in humility and vulnerability, and with the abilities that God has naturally gifted in you. As demonstrated by the life and leadership of Jesus, that combination is unbeatable.

Leadership is too important to trust to our own strengths, because as we know, even our strengths can fail us from time to time. Especially if we use them for our own machinations and not for the betterment of others and the world around us. My hope is that you will aspire to lead as Jesus led, and bring the very best that leadership has to offer.

We will fail as all frail humans do, but with failure comes humility and with humility comes authenticity which ultimately leads to credibility and trust. And what is needed in a world tired of betrayal and self-interest are leaders who are credible. May that leader be you?

NOTES

CHAPTER 1

1– Jesus Christ serves as the ultimate model of leadership for anyone in church ministry. He alone defined its parameters and the nature by which it is to be exercised. The term "Servant Leadership" has been coined for this mode of leading.

2 – Jim Collins, How the Mighty Fall. HarperCollins Publishers Inc. New York; NY, 2009. Page 8.

CHAPTER 3

1 – Tim Irwin, *Derailed: Five Lessons Learned from Catastrophic Failures in Leadership*. Thomas Nelson Publishers, Nashville Tennessee, 2009. page 165.

2 – Jim Collins, *How the Mighty Fall*, page 96.

3 – *Conquering The Enemies of Innovation: Silence and Fear* by David K. Williams and Mary Michelle Scott December 10, 2012. HBR Blog Network.

4 – John Townsend, *Now What Do I Do?: The Surprising Solution When Things Go Wrong*. Zondervan Publishing, Grand Rapids, Michigan, 2010. page 78.

5 – Seth Godin, *Linchpin: Are You Indispensable?* Penguin Books, NY, 2010. page 136.

CHAPTER 5

1 Andy Stanley, *It Came From Within: The Shocking Truth of What Lurks in the Heart.* Multnomah Publishers, Oregon: USA, page 130-134.

CHAPTER 7

1 – Two examples are Proverbs 17:6 and Isaiah 4:2. Both these passages could be translated as "glory" rather than pride. The Hebrew root denotes beauty or splendour and the context of these verses lend themselves to pride in a positive sense. The apostle Paul gives us the most comprehensive understanding of pride and its usage within the confines of Christian service in his letters 1 and 2 Corinthians, especially 2 Cor. 10-12. He frames pride in the context of boasting in the things and accomplishments of God.

2 – James Borg, *Persuasion: The Art of Influencing People.* 3d ed. Pearson Education Ltd. Harlow Gate: UK. 2010. page 234.

3 – Jim Collins, *Good to Great* (New York: Harper Business, 2001), 21.

4 – Ibid., 27.

5 – Tim Irwin, *Derailed*, 140.

6 – Collins, *How the Mighty Fall*, 29.

7 – Ibid., 20-21.

8 – Ibid., 21.

9 – The following is an excerpt from Chip and Dan Heath, *Decisive: How to Make Better Choices in Life and Work* (Toronto: Random House Canada, 2013), 92-94. For an excellent study on the dynamics of good decision making I highly encourage you to get this book.

10 – Ibid., 94.

11 – I want to acknowledge with gratitude Tim Irwin's list in *Derailed*, page 143, whose suggestions I have adopted in some form for this section.

CHAPTER 8

1 – Maurice Simon, trans., "Canticles Rabbah," in vol. 9 of *Midrash Rabbah*, ed. H. Freedman and Maurice Simon (1930; reprint: Soncino Press, 1983) p. 17.

2 – For a summary of the achievements credited to him on account of his wisdom see 1 Kings 3:12, 16-28; 4:1-33; 5:1-9; 9:18, 26-28; 10:1-9, 15-29; 2 Chronicles 1:7-12, 14-17; 2:12; Psalm 72, 127.

3 – The premise for society is one man, one woman based on Genesis 2:24. The "many" in Deuteronomy 17:17 is meant to moderate the practice of kings who took many wives to cement allegiances. Therefore, I would argue that essentially one wife is in view.

CHAPTER 9

1 – See Jeremiah 3:13; 2 Peter 2:12-22; James 2:11; Hebrews 13:4; Revelation 17:2; 18:3.

2 – Joseph Sunde, *"Timothy Keller on Work as Service vs. Idolatry,"* Acton Institute blog (12-12-12)

3 – Kent and Barbara Hughes, *Liberating the Ministry from the Success Syndrome* (Tyndale House Publishers, Wheaton: ILL., nd), 30.

4 – See Acts 17 and 19.

5 – James C. Hunter, *The World's Most Powerful Leadership Principle:How to Become a Servant Leader* (WaterBrook Press, New York, 2004), 53.

6 – Ibid., 54.

7 – Joris Lammers, Faculty of Social and Behavioral Sciences, Tilburg University, Warandelaan 2, 5037 AB Tilburg, The Netherlands E-mail: j.lammers@ uvt.nl. Abstract, Received October 22, 2010.

8 – Hunter, 54.

9 – Dave Harvey, *Rescuing Ambition* (Crossway Books, Wheaton: ILL, 2010),
10 – This is an excellent book for anyone struggling with the place of ambition
as a Christian leader.

CHAPTER 10
1 – Thesaurus supplied on my MacBook Pro

CHAPTER 11

1 – John Townsend, *Leadership Beyond Reason: How Great Leaders Succeed by
Harnessing the Power of Their Values, Feelings, and Intuition* (Thomas Nelson
Publishers, Nashville: TN, 2009), 63.

2 – Irwin, *Derailed*, 127.

3 – Ibid., 125.

4 – Ibid.

5 – Henry Cloud, *9 Things You Simply Must Do to Succeed in Love and Life*
(Integrity Publishers, Brentwood: TN., 2004), 26.

6 – John of the Cross, *Dark Night of the Soul*, 1578-1579.

7 – Mark 10:39; Luke 14:26-27; John 15:18-25, 16:1-3. See also Romans 8:17;
Galatians 6:17; Philippians 3:10.

8 – I need to credit Mark Batterson for this idiom. I heard him use it during his
session at Catalyst Conference in Atlanta, 2009.

9 – Collins, *How the Mighty Fall*, 120.

10 – Harvey, *Rescuing Ambition*, 151.

11 – Townsend, *Leadership Beyond Reason*, 89-90.

12 – John C. Maxwell, *The 21 Indispensable Qualities of a Leader: Becoming the*

Person Others Will Want to Follow (Thomas Nelson Publishers, Nashville TN:, 1999), 83.

13 – Townsend, *Leadership Beyond Reason*, 132.

CHAPTER 12

1 – Romans 1:1; Philippians 1:1; Titus 1:1.

2 – James 1:1; 2 Peter 1:1; Jude 1:1.

3 – Romans 6:14; 2 Corinthians 3:17; Galatians 2:4; 3:22; 4:5; Ephesians 1:7.

4 – Kent and Barbara Hughes, *Liberating Ministry from the Success Syndrome*, 138-139.

5 – Gordon D. Fee, *The First Epistle to the Corinthians*, in The New International Commentary on the New Testament (Eerdmans Publishing, Grand Rapids: MI, 1987), 461.

6 – Ibid.

7 – Frederick Buechner, Presbyterian minister and American writer (1926—)

CHAPTER 13

1 – The phrase was part of a message delivered by Pastor and Author Stuart Briscoe, though I do not recall what specific conference I was at or whether the phrase in question is original to him.

2 – Townsend, *Leadership Beyond Reason*, 132.

3 – Mark Cartwright, published on 02 August 2012. Ancient History Encyclopedia Website.

4 – See Romans 12:3-8; 1 Corinthians 12:1-31; Ephesians 4:11-16; 2 Timothy 1:6; 1 Peter 4:10-11.

5 – Jim Collins, *Good to Great*

6 – *Don't Let Your Strengths Become Your Weaknesses*, Harvard Business Review by Robert B. Kaiser and Robert E. Kaplan | 12:00 PM April 4, 2013

7 – That is one of the reasons Jim Collins book, *Good to Great* stood out in my mind. It brought the importance of character to bear on the success of an organization. Especially with the CEO who demonstrated humility.

8 – Andy Stanley, Catalyst Conference, Atlanta. October 2010.

9 – Brene Brown, *The Gifts of Imperfection: Let Go of Who You Think You're Supposed to Be and Embrace Who You Are* (Hazelden, MN. 2010), 72.

10 – Ibid., 70.

11 – Ibid., 72-73.

12 – Ibid., 73.

13 – Ralph Waldo Emerson, *Self-Reliance*. www.quoteoasis.com. Accessed July 15, 2013.

14 – In a October 2002 Fast Company article—*The Secret Life of the CEO: Is the Economy Just Built to Flip?*—Jim Collins http://www.jimcollins.com/article_topics/articles/the-secret-life.html, accessed July 15, 2013.

CHAPTER 14

1 – Tim Irwin, *Derailed: Five Lessons Learned from Catastrophic Failures of Leadership*

2 – From John Maxwell email newsletter Leadership Wired Feb 2013, Issue 02

3 – Stephen Brewster, *Why Success Doesn't Change People,* www.churchleaders.com. Accessed April 4, 2013. is the Creative Arts Pastor at @crosspoint_tv in Nashville, TN.

Made in the USA
Charleston, SC
28 August 2014